Connect:

High Trust Communication
for Your Success in Business and Life

(Text and Workbook)

from YourBodySoulandProsperity.com

16th Anniversary Edition, Revised

Tom Marcoux

CEO, Executive Coach

Spoken Word Strategist

Speaker-Author of 35 books

A QuickBreakthrough Publishing Edition

Other Books by Tom Marcoux:

- Discover Your Enchanted Prosperity
- Emotion-Motion Life Hacks ... for More Success and Happiness
- Relax Your Way Networking
- Darkest Secrets of Persuasion and Seduction Masters
- Darkest Secrets of Charisma
- Darkest Secrets of Negotiation Masters
- Darkest Secrets of the Film and Television Industry Every Actor Should Know
- Darkest Secrets of Making a Pitch to the Film and Television Industry
- Darkest Secrets of Film Directing
- Now You See Me – Secrets of Power Networking – More Referrals

Praise for *Connect* and Tom Marcoux:

• "Marcoux's advice on how to remain true to yourself and establish authentic rapport with clients is both insightful and reality based. Learn to establish yourself as a credible expert. This is a guide to high level relating." – Arthur P. Ciaramicoli, Ed.D., Ph.D., author, *The Curse of the Capable*

• "Concerned about networking situations? Get *Relax Your Way Networking*. Success is built on high trust relationships. Master Coach Tom Marcoux reveals secrets to increase your influence."
– Greg S. Reid, Author, *Think and Grow Rich Series*

• "Tom Marcoux has distinguished himself as a coach, speaker and self-help author. His books combine his own philosophy and teachings, as well as those of other success experts, in a highly readable and relatable manner." – Danek S. Kaus, co-author of *Power Persuasion*

Praise for Tom Marcoux's Other Work:

• "In Tom Marcoux's previous book *Your Power Path to Freedom, Success and Happiness*, you learn to make new breakthroughs to feel good, get more done, believe in yourself and enjoy each day. Feel your personal energy increase!" – Dr. JoAnn Dahlkoetter, author, *Your Performing Edge* and Coach to CEOs and Olympic Gold Medalists

• "In Tom Marcoux's *Now You See Me*, the powerful and easy-to-use ideas can make a big difference in your business and your personal relationships." – Allen Klein, author of *You Can't Ruin My Day*

• "Marcoux's book *10 Seconds to Wealth* focuses on how each of us have divine gifts that we need to understand and use to be our best when the crucial '10 seconds' occur.... He identifies the divine gifts and shares how these gifts can help us create what we want in our lives, and the wealth we want." – Linda Finkle, author of *Finding The Fork In The Road: The Art of Maximizing the Potential of Business Partnerships*

• "In *Darkest Secrets of Persuasion and Seduction Masters: How to Protect Yourself and Turn the Power to Good*, learn useful countermeasures to protect you from being darkly manipulated."
– David Barron, co-author, *Power Persuasion*

• "In *Reduce Clutter, Enlarge Your Life*, Marcoux will help you get rid of the physical and mental clutter occupying precious space in your life. You'll reclaim wasted energy, lower your stress, and find time for new opportunities." – Laura Stack, author of *Execution IS the Strategy*

Visit Tom's blog: www.BeHeardandBeTrusted.com

Tom Marcoux

CONTENTS*

* These are highlights This book includes even more material!

DEDICATION AND ACKNOWLEDGEMENTS

This book is dedicated to the terrific book and film consultant, and author Johanna E. Mac Leod. It is also dedicated to the other team members. Thanks to Linda L. Chappo and to Sun Editing & Book Design (www.SunEditWrite.com) for editing. Thanks to Johanna E. MacLeod for your editing insights and for rendering the front cover and back cover. Thanks to my father, Al Marcoux, for his concern and efforts for me. Thanks to my mother, Sumiyo Marcoux, a kind, generous soul.

Thank you to guest authors Guy Kawasaki, Dr. Fred Luskin, Marc Allen, Jeanna Gabellini, and Jay Conrad Levinson.

(For work on an earlier version of this book, thanks to Kunst + Aventur.)

Thank you to Higher Power. Thanks to our readers, audiences, clients, my graduate/college students and my team members of Tom Marcoux Media, LLC.

The best to you.

Connect: Build High Trust Relationships for Success in Business and Life

How You Can Radiate Charisma and Get What You Want

What terrific things could be in your life if you were charismatic?

Imagine if you could easily gain people's agreement and cooperation. Top professionals come across as charismatic. *The American Heritage Dictionary* defines "charisma" as "personal magnetism or charm."

A charismatic person makes each of us feel like the most important person in the room. How is this done? The charismatic person listens to others and connects with their pain.

A charismatic person often uses an effective story to engage people's emotions and open listeners to benevolent influence.

"Tom, tell me three vital parts of communicating so I can get people to trust me," Arianna, a new client, asked me. I introduced her to the W.I.N. process:

W – warm up by listening

I – intensify your story

N – nurture your personal brand

1. Warm up by listening

It all begins with listening. On the other hand, I watched my father through the years fail to listen to family members. He kills trust over and over.

We trust people who listen to us. Why? **Listening demonstrates care and respect.**

2. Intensify your story

How do we know you're trustworthy? It's through "your story." What you say plus your body language and vocal tone convey a story of *caring, competence and credibility* (I call these *the 3 Cs*). When you complain about others, you hurt your credibility. How can we trust that you'll treat us with respect? We can't.

How do we know that you care and you're competent? **What stories do you tell?** Do you speak of your blunders or do you talk about good times with "That's when I learned to _____." Here's an example of sharing one's *competence:* One of my clients said to a prospective customer: "Because I had studied graphic design, I knew to simplify the image. A number of people said that they found the cover to be eye-catching."

To really intensify your story, make it BRIEF.

This is the *16th Anniversary edition* of this book. One of my editors asked, "What have you seen in coaching people and training public speakers, these recent years?"

"It's important to be brief and powerful in your communication." I replied. Still, listening is vital. I say, *"When you're listening, you're winning."* After you've listened, then you respond in a targeted, bite-sized message.

To refine your point, consider developing a "headline"

that is 140 characters (or less)—like a Tweet that we use at Twitter.

3. Nurture your personal brand

Your personal brand is the answer to the question: "What are you best known for?" It's what people can count on you to do. In a sense it is your reputation. I have guided clients to add "T.H.O.R." to their personal brand. By T.H.O.R. I mean you come across as *Trustworthy, Helpful, Organized and Respectful.*

Another part of your personal brand relates to *Authenticity, Evidence and Experience* (what I call A.E.E.—or "A double-E"). When you speak authentically, another person can sense it. As an Executive Coach and Spoken Word Strategist, I guide my clients to highlight their *experience.* I emphasize: "You are the expert about your own experience. Tell stories based on what you learned. Avoid repeating clichéd stories."

Success and Fulfillment are Built on High Trust Relationships

This book will help you communicate authentically and in ways to develop warm relationships.

People do not care how much you know until they know how much you care. – *John C. Maxwell*

A charismatic person expresses compelling messages. Dictionary.com defines "compelling" as "to force or drive, especially to a course of action … to overpower … to have a powerful and irresistible effect, influence." We want to overpower inertia, low moods, and procrastination. We want to take action consistently to create the best possible situations in our own lives.

An interviewer said to me, "I'm not comfortable with that

word in the definition: 'force.'"

"All right, let's **focus on having a good intention first**," I replied. "Instead of force, let's aim **to 'move'** a person's emotions. "For example, when I was ten years old, my piano teacher knew how to persuade me to practice. She helped me see how much I improved when I practiced. She moved my emotions so that I could feel and enjoy the benefits I was getting. She also cleverly had me practice a song that I really wanted to play."

In essence, my piano teacher was a compelling communicator. She was heard and trusted by me. And that's what you'll learn how to do in this book.

How much would your life improve if you could easily get people to say yes to you? What if you could easily get them to want to say yes?

- "Yes! You're hired. The job is yours."
- "Yes! Here's your raise and promotion."
- "Yes! I'll marry you."
- "Yes! Here's $200,000 to develop your entrepreneurial idea."
- "Yes! I'll buy your product."

What if you could get what you really want—faster than you ever imagined?

That was both the opportunity and the problem for my client Sarah. She confessed, "I need to improve my communication skills."

"How would that give you what you really want?" I asked.

For a moment, she frowned in thought.

"And what do you really want?"

"A raise and a promotion!" she said with sudden clarity.

"What would that take?"

"My boss would have to trust me with higher profile

assignments."

In essence, Sarah didn't just want to improve her communication skills; she wanted to be heard and be trusted. With my guidance, Sarah learned to use the skills found in this book. She learned methods to increase her confidence, speak well to authority, and feel higher self-esteem.

I have helped thousands of clients and audience members become great communicators. In fact, an earlier version of this book functioned as a textbook by Cogswell Polytechnical College and is included in that college's time capsule. *[As mentioned, we've reached this 16th Anniversary Edition.]*

The capsule is set to be opened in 2100. Even in 2100, the timeless principles of warm and trustworthy communication will be valuable.

In this book, we will cover story after story that highlight how many, including billionaires and millionaires, communicate successfully to make things happen. You will also learn directly from the articles and comments of a number of other great communicators.

This book is filled with principles that can help you relate to people on a higher level of connection and cooperation.

As to methods there may be a million and then some, but principles are few. The man who grasps principles can successfully select his own methods. The man who tries methods, ignoring principles, is sure to have trouble. – Ralph Waldo Emerson

For compelling communication, you need to do two things:

1. Seize the attention
2. Create a connection

We want our communication to be *not* merely pleasant, but compelling. We want people to cooperate with us, to take action in the direction we're proposing. To help you make this year the best year of your life so far, we will explore the C.O.M.P.E.L. process.

C - Connect with the listener's pain

O - Open with genuineness

M - Maximize leverage

P - Pull with a story

E - Ease

L - Lift

"Be so good—they can't ignore you," said writer-actor-comedian Steve Martin in response to the question, "How do you gain big success?" With this book, you will become so good at influencing people. And, I will add, be so trustworthy that they want to do *for* you.

Let's move forward and learn how to be charismatic and influential ...

Connect with the Listener's Pain

Where does it hurt? Did your attention go to your body? Did you feel tension in your neck area?

To make your message compelling, you need to uncover your listener's pain.

Ask someone what he or she wants. The easiest way for the person to reply is to say, "What I don't want is to stay in this job. Here's what I do not like in my current situation." The person talks about what causes pain.

What I have in my heart must come out; that is the reason I compose. – Ludwig van Beethoven

Beethoven reminds us that what is in our hearts must come out. Similarly, as great communicators we need to help our listener express his or her heartfelt pains and desires. By helping your listener identify "where it hurts," you can help her achieve a transformation.

The power of transformation reminds me of the journey of Gay Hendricks, the bestselling author of *Five Wishes* and cofounder of The Hendricks Institute. Years ago, when he was a 300-pound tobacco addict in a horrible marriage, he felt the need to reinvent himself. Gay was blocked. His blockage was made of conflicted feelings: he couldn't decide whether to continue studying in the University of New Hampshire counseling program or follow his desire to be a writer. Dwight Webb, an insightful professor of his, suggested, "Why not write about counseling?" Was there any reason Gay could not put his feelings and inner experiences into poems and articles connected with his profession? The answer was that *he could do both things* he loved. He could pursue psychological counseling and writing. Gay's poems were published in counseling journals and caught the eye of a professor at Stanford University, who helped Gay gain a fellowship to that institution for his doctorate. Gay went on to a 25-year academic career and wrote over 20 books. (He also transformed to a fit, 180-pound frame, over six feet tall.)

When I contacted Gay a while ago, I discovered that he had found fulfillment as a screenwriter-filmmaker and as a seminar leader through The Hendricks Institute. Gay's journey shows that it is an "and" universe, not a "this or that" universe. [I wrote the book *The Hidden Power of the AND-Universe*.] The point is that Gay's professor Dwight Webb provided great coaching. He listened to Gay's pain and shared a new way to view the situation.

The only service a friend can really render is to keep up your courage by holding up to you a mirror in which you can see a noble image of yourself. – George Bernard Shaw

When you really want to be heard and be trusted, focus on something that will benefit the other person. Be the person's friend. Take the appropriate actions to help him or her.

With a number of my clients, we focus on the transition from novice salesperson to coach-to-action. As George Bernard Shaw points out, you as the coach can hold a friendly mirror up to your listener, who will then be able to see a noble image of the self. This noble image can inspire the listener to agree to whatever you're offering. And as the coach, you can help the person enjoy more in life and work.

It is above all by the imagination that we achieve perception and compassion and hope. – Ursula LeGuin

First, connect with the listener's pain. Then, with the knowledge you have gained, you can focus on helping. You can help people imagine a better personal future.

People in general are starved for the experience of being heard.
– Gordon Livingston, M.D.

Get what you want by giving people what they crave: to be heard.

Principle: Connect with the listener's pain and show that you have the remedy.

Power Question: How can you gently ask questions that allow you to identify the listener's pain?*

NOTE: * *To get the maximum benefit from this book, devote at least 20 seconds to writing down an answer to each Power Question in your personal journal (or in this book).*

Open with Genuineness

When you are content to be simply yourself and don't compare or compete, everybody will respect you. – Lao-tzu

"We don't need you to be perfect; we need you to be genuine," I say to my clients/audiences who seek to be better public speakers and pitch-givers.

Do what you said you were going to do, when you said you were going to do it, in exactly the way you said you were going to do it. You won't ever get any better business advice than that. Be there when you said you would be there. Deliver when you said you would deliver. Call when you said you would call. Be a person who can be counted on by keeping his word every time.

– Larry Winget

Have you ever been afraid that when you are giving a speech, your mind might go blank or you might lose your place? The solution is *be genuine.*

When I coach CEOs and company presidents in how to give speeches, I help them express genuineness. This helps the CEO connect with the audience and motivate team members.

The lesson of recovery applies whether you are talking with one person or speaking to a group.

4 Recovery Methods:

1. If you mispronounce a word, say, "Oh, I don't use that word every day." Then slowly say the word again.

2. If you lose your place, respond with something like, "My train of thought just derailed. I'm waiting for a crane." The idea is to pick a gentle phrase that might include a bit of humor.

3. If you make an error, remark, "That's not what I meant to say. What I meant was … "

4. If English is your second language and you see that people haven't understood what you've just said, *use a*

synonym. One of my clients mispronounced "result." I invited the client to say "outcome."

During one class, when I was teaching the method of saying, "My train of thought just derailed," I suggested that the students come up with their own comments. My graduate student Joseph Hsieh suggested, "Oh, I need a moment; my brain doesn't have enough RAM."

Ah, the first step in humility: Listening. – Dr. Michael Bernard Beckwith

A crucial part of genuineness is true caring & listening

Listening is one of the best ways to show how important we feel another person is. To listen well, we need to avoid listening blockers. (Authors Paul J. Donoghue and Mary E. Siegel write about the habits that block listening.)

Listening blockers

1. Judging - A friend talks about her ex-husband again and again. You are thinking: "Enough already! Can't you move on?"

2. Defending - Your roommate suggests that you do more to help keep the place clean. You yell back, "I do chores around here! Two weeks ago, I … "

3. "Me, too!"—One Up – One says, "Yes, finals are tough for *me, too*. In fact, I have eight classes." This becomes "one up" (or "one better") if the other person has only five classes.

The solution to our own listening blockers is to observe our behavior. If you find yourself responding with judging, defending or *"Me, too!—One Up,"* pause. Be quiet. Then say something like,

1. So, how do you feel about the situation?

2. That must have been frustrating for you.

It often helps to ask a gentle question that returns the conversational spotlight to the other person.

What do we live for, if it is not to make life less difficult for each other?– George Eliot (pen name of Mary Ann Evans)

Principle: Show your genuineness and put the person at ease.

Power Questions: How can you reveal that you are genuine? What brief stories demonstrate how much you care about people and perform supportive actions?

_____

_____

_____

_____

_____

Maximize Leverage

What do most of us want? We want the greatest benefit for the least effort. In fact, for many individuals, getting something for nothing would be just fine. Others realize that giving and receiving is a natural law.

This is where leverage comes in. The person you're talking with wants to avoid effort and pain—and still gain benefits.

Show how your ideas and solutions maximize the person's leverage. At one conference I attended, a tax accountant said that he would show us how to gain $5,000 a year with only a bit of extra effort. He had our attention. How can we find out what will truly gain the attention of our listener?

Inspiration usually comes during work, rather than before it.
– Madeleine L'Engle

Let's do the work. Write down two quick responses to each of these questions (on the lines below):

- What is most important to my customer (my friend? my spouse?)
- What does the person want?
- What does the person want to avoid?
- How can my solution give the person the greatest benefit for the least effort?

Write some first thoughts that answer the above questions here:

_____

_____

_____

_____

_____

As stated in Madeleine's quote, it is during the process of writing the answers to these questions (doing the work) that we will often find the inspiration.

Questions help you discover what matters most to your listener.

Principle: Show how your solution provides the person with the greatest benefit for the least effort (leverage).

Power Questions: What is it about your solution that provides the greatest benefit? How can you ask questions to discover what the person most desires?

Pull with a Story

"Tell me a story!" Millions of children throughout the world say this every day. A story gives us an experience. The story reaches us on our subconscious and emotional levels. The story goes around people's natural resistance.

We have been conditioned to respond favorably to stories. With a dash of suspense, tension, and release, your story can influence your listener.

If you can dream it, you can do it. – Walt Disney

It all comes down to the story you tell yourself. – Tom Marcoux

Facts go in our brains. Stories go in our hearts. – Sandra Bloch

A good story …
1. Begins with a grabber
2. Has suspense
3. Has vivid details and a "goal"
4. Includes word pictures
5. Ends with "What I learned was … "
6. Has a call to action

I call the above details: The 6 Elements of a Good Story.

A word picture creates an image. To a friend who likes puppies, I said, "When I'm waiting for you, I feel like a puppy on a raft in the middle of the Atlantic Ocean, never knowing whether a rescue ship is going to appear." My comment touched her heart.

A story with a goal gives us the chance to earn the ending. We go through the trials and suffering along with the main character.

Character cannot be developed in ease and quiet.

Only through experience of trial and suffering

can the soul be strengthened, vision cleared,
ambition inspired, and success achieved. – Helen Keller

We want to earn the happy ending. We want to see how the hero with good intentions struggles and then earns the positive outcome.

Using 6 Elements of a Good Story, write down your first ideas for a story that can help you gain cooperation from someone:

_____

_____

_____

_____

_____

A story helps you make your point powerfully. **The following anecdote is one of the signature stories I tell my audiences.**

"We need to be careful about the stories we tell ourselves—and the stories we tell others. At one point, my wife and I went on the Disney Cruise. We went to refresh ourselves, and I also went on the cruise to find more stories. I felt that I needed a story. I need an adventure.

"When I was younger, I did stunts. For a feature film, I held onto the hood of a speeding truck, a cherry-red classic Chevy truck going 63 miles an hour. Not any more! So now I need an adventure.

"Let's go on a cruise and go snorkeling for the first time!" It looked good on paper. So I go snorkeling with my sweetheart. It's the Bahamas, and it's 83 degrees at eight o'clock in the morning. It's hot, so she tells me that the water will be warm. But the water is relatively cold. And I discover what happens in cold water. First thing I learn: What is worse than a cramp in your right leg?

"A cramp in both legs," says an audience member.

"Yes! You're right here with me. A cramp in both legs. So I start to use my arms. Thank goodness for Red Cross swimming lessons! I do the sidestroke. And my sweetheart – yes, she's better at snorkeling her first time than I am. (Women in the audience laugh.) She's towing me a little bit, too. That's comforting.

"Eventually, we get back to the ship and our cabin. And I discover the second thing that happens in cold water: things shrink! (Audience chuckles.) My hand has shrunk. My wedding-ring finger has shrunk. (Audible gasps.)

"My wedding ring is now lost in hundreds of yards of water and sand. My wedding band is gone! And I'm thinking, "All right, I teach this stuff. I've taught Comparative Religion for over 14 years at Academy of Art University. My ring has gone back to the universe. Someone will find it who needs it more than I. (Audience laughs.)

"I discovered: All men make mistakes; married men just find out about it sooner. (Audience laughs).

"My wife tells me, "You do not go into water with jewelry on!" I am not into jewelry—and now jewelry is not on me!

"So I call up the ship's Guest Services and say, "My wedding ring is somewhere in hundreds of yards of sand and water." The person says that I can come by and fill out the form. There's always a form. There's a form for losing your wedding ring.

"The next day, I go to the Guest Services desk. "I'm here to fill out the form. I lost my wedding ring."

"Where did you lose it?" the guy asks me.

"I was on the island tram. And I was at the snorkeling lagoon … "

"Is this your ring?" (Audience gasps.)

"And here is the ring. (I hold up my hand with the wedding ring.)

"To me, it is a miracle. And it reminds me of what *Albert Einstein said:*

"There are two ways to live: you can live as if nothing is a miracle; you can live as if everything is a miracle."

"We have a choice. And so, what are the stories you are telling yourself? What are the stories you tell others?

Are you telling yourself stories so that you can experience more success and happiness?

You can see how this snorkeling-adventure story illustrates my point about the stories we tell ourselves and others. Be careful about the stories you tell yourself and the stories you tell others.

Tell good stories–miraculous stories.

Remember to pull the listener in with a good story.

Principle: Use a story to eliminate resistance.

Power Question: What stories can seize the attention of your listener?

Ease

What do you wish was easier in your life? Imagine how it would be if the person you were talking with thought you could bring ease into his or her life. This person would likely be receptive to your comments.

As a verb, "ease" implies going forward gently: to ease into something. Dictionary.com defines ease (as a noun) as "freedom from labor, pain, physical annoyance, concern, anxiety, difficulty, great effort, stiffness, constraint, formality or financial need." Ease relates to "tranquil rest; comfort; a quiet state of mind; and plenty."

Wow! Let's have some of that! To set a person at ease is a powerful way to be heard and trusted.

The twin killers of success are impatience and greed. - Jim Rohn

Don't rush the person you're talking with. Show patience. The point is to make it easy for the person to buy your product or idea.

We make things easy by asking a gentle question and listening to the potential customer.

For example, one salesman approached me by saying, "I know a lot about your work." And without showing any patience, he launched right into his pitch.

I did *not* buy the advertising he was offering.

It would have helped if he had replaced his supposed "efficiency" by saying something gentle and easy. He could have said, "Our advertising process reaches four major cities in your target area. What message would you like to bring to those people?" Then he could have listened to my response. This would have made the process easy. I would have replied with something like, "That's a good question. I would like them to know about my new book, and that I'll be appearing at X and Y, and I am offering a special value and discount with … " A gentle question would have made it easy for me to "sell myself " on the idea of using his type of advertising. Great communicators know to avoid rushing the person they're talking with. Again, show patience and make your listener feel at ease.

Principle: Set the person at ease, and you will gain cooperation.

Power Questions: How can you set the person at ease? How can you ask a gentle question and then listen? (Remember, listening demonstrates that you are trustworthy and that the speaker's well-being is important to you.)

Lift

What four words have lifted the hearts of millions of people for decades? Martin Luther King, Jr., said them: "I have a dream." I'm mentioning this again because great communicators tell inspiring stories to themselves and other people.

Dr. Wayne Dyer, the late bestselling author, told how he left the security of the bimonthly paychecks he received as a college professor to go out on his own. In 1976, he decided that he would buy a large number of copies of his first book, entitled *Your Erroneous Zones*, appear on local media shows and leave his books at stores across America on consignment. He used his own savings to purchase the books and pay travel expenses for his wife, his daughter, and himself. As the months went by, the number of interviews he was asked to give rose to 15 a day, and bookstores began to reorder the books from his publisher.

A publicity expert had told Wayne that he would not sell enough books without a network television appearance, but Wayne proved him wrong. In one year, Wayne accomplished what seemed impossible: without his making one major television network appearance, his book debuted on the *New York Times* Best Seller List at position number eight. Wayne concludes, "I received more money in the first year I was out on my own without the security of a regular paycheck than I had in the entire 36 years of my life before then."

Many people have succeeded and later said, "I didn't know that it couldn't be done." In the same way, you can use the secrets and methods in this book to give you the edge you need to make dreams come true. It all starts with having a dream. A dream can lift our souls and fill us with the energy to take action.

Principle: Lift people's hearts. Mention a dream and express your enthusiasm.

Power Question: How can you demonstrate that what you're doing or offering is exciting and full of powerful benefits?

Part I, Section 2
How Billionaires and Millionaires Use
C. O. M. P. E. L. Principles

Here are the C.O.M.P.E.L. principles once again:
C - Connect with the Listener's Pain
O - Open with Genuineness
M - Maximize Leverage
P - Pull with a Story
E - Ease
L - Lift

Bill Gates uses the principle *Maximize Leverage*. He said, "The first rule of any technology used in a business is that automation applied to an efficient operation will magnify the efficiency. The second is that automation applied to an inefficient operation will magnify the inefficiency." And, "As we look ahead into the next century, leaders will be those who empower others." And, "Often you have to rely on intuition." Bill Gates uses the principle *Connect with the Listener's Pain*. "If you show people the problems and you show people the solutions they will be moved to act."

Oprah Winfrey uses the principles of *Open with Genuineness* and *Connect with the Listener's Pain*. After the author James Frey said on the "Larry King Live" show that he had made up some of his book, *A Million Little Pieces*, Oprah apologized for a phone call she had made to the show in which she supported the book. Soon after that, on her own television show Oprah apologized to her national audience for defending James Frey. "I made a mistake and I left the impression that the truth does not matter, and I am deeply sorry about that because that is not what I believe," she said.

When Frey later appeared on her show, Oprah said to him, "It is difficult for me to talk to you because I really feel duped ... More importantly, I feel you betrayed millions of readers ... As I sit here today, I don't know what is true, and I don't know what isn't."

It was reported that during her interview with James Frey, Oprah was near tears. Her audience gasped, moved by her obvious sincerity and regret.

Being genuine and apologizing sincerely is compelling. It inspires trust. Oprah knows the power her book club wields. When she selected Frey's book for the club, over three million copies were sold. Since then, Oprah has been careful to avoid memoirs because she feels that publishers do not properly vet the books. Oprah's sincere good will captivates her audiences.

Jack Canfield uses the principle of *Maximize Leverage*. He said, "There are two things that build self-esteem. One is quality of relationships, where you feel lovable and you're making a difference in the lives of others. And the other is achieving things ... People who ask confidently get more than those who are hesitant and uncertain. When you've figured out what you want to ask for, do it with certainty, boldness and confidence." Jack and his partner, Mark Victor Hansen, used the principle of *Ease*. They envisioned their book, *Chicken Soup for the Soul*, topping the *New York Times* Best Seller List. They cut out a copy of the list from the newspaper and modified it, adding the name of their book to the top of that list. As a team, they did double the number of media interviews either of them could have done alone. They encouraged each other consistently.

Brian Tracy used the principle of *Lift* as he raised himself from poverty. He said, "Your decision to be, have and do something out of the ordinary entails facing difficulties that are out of the ordinary as well. Sometimes your greatest asset is simply your ability to stay with it longer than anyone else." Brian Tracy learned how to do real estate deals by reading every book on real estate that was available at the public library. Today, he still reads hundreds of books and magazine articles to keep his knowledge current and increase his effectiveness. This inspired me; in 2015, I read 74 books.

Tony Robbins uses the principle of *Connect with Your Listener's Pain.* He said, "In life you need either inspiration or desperation." And, "When you are grateful, fear disappears and abundance appears." And, "It's not the events of our lives that shape us, but our beliefs as to what those events mean." Also, "One reason so few of us achieve what we truly want is that we never direct our focus; we never concentrate our power. Most people dabble their way through life, never deciding to master anything in particular … Take control of your consistent emotions and begin to consciously and deliberately reshape your daily experience of life." Finally, "The way we communicate with others and with ourselves ultimately determines the quality of our lives."

Warren Buffet uses the principle of *Lift*. He said, "Someone's sitting in the shade today because someone planted a tree a long time ago." Also, "It's better to hang out with people better than you. Pick out associates whose behavior is better than yours, and you'll drift in that direction." And, "A public-opinion poll is no substitute for thought." Also, "It takes 20 years to build a reputation and five minutes to ruin it. If you think about that, you'll do things differently … If you can tell me who your heroes are, I can tell you how you're going to turn out in life." Also, "I call investing the greatest business in the world because you never have to swing. You stand at the plate. The pitcher throws you General Motors at 47! U.S. Steel at 39! and nobody calls a strike on you. There's no penalty except opportunity lost. All day you wait for the pitch you like. Then when the fielders are asleep, you step up and hit it."

Journalist Larry Kanter described Warren Buffet's strategy: "Ignoring both macroeconomic trends and Wall Street fashions, [Warren Buffet] looks for undervalued companies with low overhead costs, high growth potential, strong market share and low price-to-earnings ratios, and then waits for the rest of the world to catch up."

Suze Orman uses *Connect with the Listener's Pain*. She said, "A big part of financial freedom is having your heart and mind free from worry about the what-ifs of life."

And, "People first, then money, then things." Also, "In all realms of life it takes courage to stretch your limits, express your power, and fulfill your potential … it's no different in the financial realm." She adds, "Courage is the ability to face danger, difficulty, uncertainty or pain without being overcome by fear or being deflected from a chosen course of action." She wrote, "Truth creates money, lies destroy it."

Steve Jobs used the principle *Maximize Leverage*. "The only way to do great work is to love what you do. If you haven't found it yet, keep looking. Don't settle. As with all matters of the heart, you'll know when you find it." Also, "When Apple came up with the Mac, IBM was spending at least 100 times more on R&D. It's not about money. It's about the people you have, how you're led, and how much you get it ... It's really hard to design products by focus groups ... A lot of times, people don't know what they want until you show it to them." Steve Jobs also used the principle of *Lift:* "Be a yardstick of quality. Some people aren't used to an environment where excellence is expected ... Sometimes when you innovate, you make mistakes. It is best to admit them quickly, and get on with improving your other innovations."

Walt Disney focused on the principle of *Lift.* He said, "I don't want the public to see the world they live in while they're in the [Disneyland] Park. I want them to feel they're in another world ... I would rather entertain and hope that people learned something than educate people and hope they were entertained." And, "I believe in being an innovator ... We keep moving forward, opening new doors, and doing new things, because we're curious and curiosity keeps leading us down new paths." Walt also said, "Laughter is America's most important export."

Richard Branson uses the principle of *Maximize Leverage:* "A business has to be involving, it has to be fun, and it has to exercise your creative instincts ... If you can run one business well, you can run any business well." Also, "I want Virgin to be as well-known around the world as Coca-Cola ... I have enjoyed life a lot more by saying yes than by saying no." Branson also noted, "Business opportunities are like buses, there's always another one coming ... I never get the accountants in before I start up a business. It's done on gut feeling ... "

Branson explains, "I have always lived my life by thriving

on opportunity and adventure. Some of the best ideas come out of the blue, and you have to keep an open mind to see their virtue ... Fantasizing about the future is one of my favorite pastimes ... My biggest motivation? Just to keep challenging myself. I see life almost like one long University education that I never had—every day I'm learning something new."

Bonus Section:
Develop Your Charisma by Nurturing Yourself

"How can I be more attractive when I first meet people?" my client Adam asked.

"You need reserves of energy. One way you can develop this is by nurturing yourself," I replied.

I first addressed this with the below article at my blog BeHeardandBeTrusted.com:

Act Like Your Own Best Friend

"Is there one action that could make a big difference in my finally breaking out to real success?" my client Veronica asked.

During our conversation, I brought some principles to her attention.

- Act like your own best friend
- Break out of the perfectionism trap
- Answer "What will bring you peace?"

1. Act like your own best friend

"My mother hates my lamb stew," my friend Cindy said.

"Wait a minute. Doesn't your mother simply dislike lamb

at all?" I asked.

"Yeah, but–"

"I hear your 'yeah, but.' Would you pause for a moment?" I asked.

"Okay."

"I've heard you do this before. You express things in the manner of 'Cindy's at fault' or 'Cindy's work is not good enough.' To put it in few words, you're *not* being kind to yourself."

I invite you to be a friend to yourself. What does that entail? **Be kind to yourself.** Listen to see if you're needlessly berating yourself and—STOP THAT.

Encourage yourself.

Now it's your turn. Are you being a good friend to yourself? Do you take good care of yourself? What can you do to strengthen yourself? How about enough sleep, good nutrition, appropriate exercise—and time away from negative people?

2. Break out of the perfectionism trap

Recently, I started three different blog articles. I didn't feel that they measured up. Then I caught myself and said, "Break out of the perfectionism trap."

It's better to **Set Criteria for Excellence.**

My criteria for excellence includes a) tell the truth and b) express something that can help the reader.

Good. I can do that. Hence, we have this section here.

Now it's your turn. Are your preventing yourself from getting something done because you're caught up in perfectionism? What would you choose to do if you Set Criteria for Excellence?

3. Answer "What will bring you peace?"

At one point, I was working with a client who felt frustrated and surprised that her recent big accomplishment didn't bring the happiness she was expecting.

I said, "Don't hesitate. Tell me right now. What will bring you peace, Serena?"

"I don't know— "

"Don't tell me a story. Just talk," I said.

"Oh. All right. Uh, a walk in trees."

"Trees. Got it."

"Reading. In a hot bath. Kicking back," Serena said.

"Good. Continue."

"Maybe going back to the yoga class."

"Continue."

"Knitting?"

"Are you asking me? Or telling me?"

"Knitting."

"In silence? With music?"

"Sometimes in quiet. Sometimes with music," Serena said, now smiling.

"Okay. Send me an email after you've done one of those things in the next three to four hours."

"I like this!" Serena said.

Now it's your turn. What will bring you peace? What will you put in your day planner and actually do?

Remember:

- Act like your own best friend
- Break out of the perfectionism trap
- Answer "What will bring you peace?"

Part II, Section 1
Great Communicators Handle Fear

What if you could handle fear and get it out of your way? How amazing and fulfilling would your life be?

As you learn how to handle fear, you will become someone who is heard and trusted. Top professionals are heard and trusted because people believe that they can handle fear with grace and strength.

The greatest communicators have a special advantage: they are skilled in communicating with themselves. They talk to themselves in ways that get them into action.

How do you talk to yourself about your fears? Many people have become paralyzed by fear. If they have read some idea about how to deal with their fear, trying to apply that idea merely frustrates them.

Fear defeats more people than any other one thing in the world.
– Ralph Waldo Emerson

The good news is that this section will help you work with the fear and transform it into something you can use to lift your life to a higher level of success and fulfillment.

Courage is not the absence of fear, but rather the judgment that something else is more important than fear. – Meg Cabot

What could be more important than fear? Living your life with joy and fulfillment.

I don't believe people are looking for the meaning of life as much as they are looking for the experience of being alive.
– Joseph Campbell

In this section, I will share two powerful processes for handling fear:

1. Reduce Risk
2. Power Thought/Physiology Method (the Three-Fs)

Fear affects much of what we do and what we avoid doing. Some of us are truly diminished by the fear of being hurt. But if we have ways to deal with pain, we become stronger. We experience more freedom.

This discussion about fear is vital if you want to be a great communicator, someone who is heard and trusted. Great communicators deal with their own fears and they help their audiences handle fear, too. Great communicators guide audiences to move beyond fear to real freedom.

Here are Dr. Fred Luskin's comments on how to free ourselves from pain by engaging in the process of forgiveness.

Guest Article

Nine Steps of Forgiveness
by Dr. Fred Luskin

My book *Forgive for Good: A Proven Prescription for Health and Happiness* is a primer on how to make peace when things you choose or things chosen for you do not work out well. When painful things happen you have a choice. I teach people to make more forgiving choices. I do this because I understand that as a function of life everyone will have painful experiences as well as pleasant ones. It is a singular power to be able to handle what comes your way without getting lost in blame and suffering. We do not know what the game of life has in store but we do know that forgiveness is one way that provides strength to get back into the game.

As Director of the Stanford Forgiveness Projects my forgiveness methodology has been tested and shown to be successful through a number of research projects. We have demonstrated that forgiveness can reduce stress, blood pressure, anger, depression, hurt, and increase optimism, hope, compassion, physical vitality, and forgiveness. We have worked with people who have been lied to, cheated, abandoned, physically injured, beaten, abused or had their children murdered. Forgiveness training made a significant difference in many of their lives. What follows is our nine step method of teaching and becoming forgiving.

Nine Steps to Forgiveness

1. Know exactly how you feel about what happened and be able to articulate what about the situation is not OK. Then, tell a couple of trusted people about your experience.

2. Make a commitment to yourself to do what you have to do to feel better. Forgiveness is for you and not for anyone else.

3. Forgiveness does not necessarily mean reconciliation with the person that upset you, or condoning of their action. What you are after is to find peace. Forgiveness can be defined as the "peace and understanding that come from blaming that which has hurt you less, taking the life experience less personally, and amending your grievance story."

4. Get the right perspective on what is happening. Recognize that your primary distress is coming from the hurt feelings, thoughts, and physical upset you are suffering now, not what offended you or hurt you two minutes—or ten years—ago.

5. At the moment you feel upset practice stress management to soothe your body's flight or fight response.

6. Give up expecting things from other people, or your life, that they do not choose to give you. Recognize the "unenforceable rules" you have for your health or how you or other people must behave. Remind yourself that you can hope for health, love, friendship and prosperity, and work hard to get them. However, you will suffer when you demand these things occur when you do not have the power

to make them happen.

7. Put your energy into looking for another way to get your positive goals met than through the experience that has hurt you. I call this step finding your positive intention. Instead of mentally replaying your hurt seek out new ways to get what you want.

8. Remember that a life well lived is your best revenge. Instead of focusing on your wounded feelings, and thereby giving the person who caused you pain power over you, learn to look for the love, beauty, and kindness around you. Appreciate what you have more than attending to what you do not have.

9. Amend your grievance story to remind you of the heroic choice to forgive.

– Dr. Fred Luskin, author of **Forgive for Good** *and* **Forgive for Love** *www.LearningToForgive.com*

When we know how to deal with great pain, we can free up our personal energy. With more energy, we can take our lives and our businesses to higher levels.

The most successful people, those who enjoy personal fulfillment, are skillful in the ways they handle fear. They realize this truth:

We fear the thing we want the most. – Dr. Robert Anthony

Part II, Section 2
Reduce Risk

What lies below the paralysis many people face when confronted with tough decisions? It is fear. They think, "I'll be hurt."

You block your dream when you allow your fear to grow bigger than your faith. – Mary Manin Morrissey

What is the faith you need? Faith that you will adapt. How can you have this faith? You prepare. **Courage is easier when you're prepared.**

Now I'll share with you powerful ways to prepare, with the Reduce Risk System.*

(* *I note that this process manages the risk of failure by managing fear, not risk per se. This process reduces perceived risk, thereby enabling one to take effective action.*)

The most powerful way to handle fear is to communicate effectively with yourself.

Researchers note that we communicate with ourselves constantly throughout the day. Random thoughts keep arising: "That worked," or "I can't do that because ... " Unfortunately, much of what we think is fear-based.

Author Gene Bedell identified five buying anxieties:
1. Reluctance to give up options
2. Fear of making a mistake
3. Social pressures
4. Fear of losing
5. Perceived cost

What does this have to do with handling fear? A lot! When you handle each of these five buying anxieties, you empower yourself to take action. So I created a system to reduce risk. We use the R.E.D.U.C.E. process:

R – Revise options
E – Envision solutions to mistakes
D – Disengage from the fear of loss
U – Unleash yourself from social pressures
C – Cover the cost
E – Engage rehearsal

To show how the process works, I will tell you how my client Stephanie went from paralysis and fear about hiring an editor for her new book to taking effective action.

Revise Options

Handle the reluctance to give up options

"What if I pick the wrong editor?" Stephanie asked, her voice choked by fear. She thought she had only two options: to pick the best editor or to fail by picking the wrong editor.

Stephanie's black-and-white thinking was keeping her paralyzed. I helped her realize that she could revise her thinking about her options and see that she had more than two choices.

Stephanie converted the idea of "best editor" into "good or excellent editor." She reduced the negative emotional charge carried by her fear of failure. With this viewpoint, she could take action.

Stephanie set up a four-step plan:

1. Identify her criteria.

2. Contact the local editors' association.

3. Interact with 10 editors.

4. Request to see 500-word samples of the work of three prospective editors.

Luck affects everything. Let your hook be always cast; in the pool where you least expect it, there will be a fish. – Ovid

An old phrase says, "Success goes to the activist." By taking action, Stephanie moved through her fear toward a better life. The life she envisions includes ultimately becoming an author of bestselling books. She needs to learn her craft first, so she must find an excellent editor for her current book.

Once, an interviewer mentioned to me, "You have been talking about revising options. Some of my friends face too many options. In fact, they complain, 'I don't have one focus. I wish I had wanted to become a doctor or something like that. At least I would have focused on one thing. But I don't like any one thing that much. What can I do?'"

I replied, "I help a number of clients and audience members who are confronted with this dilemma of too many options and 'I'm feeling not passionate about anything in particular.' We focus on two useful strategies."

Strategies to handle the "I don't have one focus" problem

1. If you're an idea-person, team up with "implementers."

2. Keep a few projects progressing simultaneously.

The idea-person teams up with " implementers"

Some people are idea-people. They can come up with good ideas, but they're not interested in becoming experts at the tasks that are involved in implementing those ideas. It helps when idea-people team up with implementers.

Some people are "starters." Implementers are "finishers." They get a lot of joy out of finishing a task well. For example, a book designer I know loves to complete projects to his standard of excellence. He is an implementer (among other talents). I have no interest in learning how to use typesetting software, so it's best for me to hire someone who will do a terrific job with the typesetting. I'm an idea-person who loves to write.

Keep a few parallel projects progressing simultaneously

For those people who say that they get bored easily with just one project, the solution is to have a few parallel projects progressing simultaneously. This keeps the person feeling constantly renewed because she can rotate the projects.

For example, at this moment I am involved with these projects:

1. I am typing the words of this book (project one).

2. My graphic novel illustrator revises the design of the villain for my graphic novel *Jack AngelSword* (project two).

3. My office team leader sets up my next speaking engagements. (project three).

One interviewer asked me, "Aren't you spreading yourself too thin?"

I replied, "Because I have a number of dreams, I have devoted time and energy to learning the skill of delegating. So my projects can progress while I'm not there."

The important idea is to keep vigilant, watching for one project to become "red-hot." The way work flows is that at certain times, some projects become popular or gain an almost miraculous momentum. At that point, it is wise to pull back to some degree from the other projects and put the appropriate attention, money, time, and resources into the red-hot project.

Envision Solutions to Mistakes
Handle the fear of making a mistake

My client Stephanie tells herself that at the worst, she could hire a second editor to correct the first editor's errors. That is a solution. This is a strategic plan because Stephanie realizes that she can recover from a mistake. She has a plan.

To live a creative life, we must lose our fear of being wrong.
– Joseph Chilton Pearce

Let's bring this down to financial considerations. Based on her last book's performance, Stephanie thinks she can make a profit of at least $3,000. (And she has a plan to market this new book in more profitable ways.) So if the first editor makes a mistake and Stephanie must hire a second editor at $700, she still clears $1,600.

The solution here is to prepare for what could go wrong. Make sure that you can be well even if you go through a bumpy time.

Aim for success, not perfection. Never give up your right to be wrong, because then you will lose the ability to learn new things and move forward with your life. – Dr. David M. Burns

Disengage from the Fear of Loss

Handle the fear of losing

Let the fear of danger be a spur to prevent it; he that fears not, gives advantage to the danger. – Francis Quarles

The solution is to think the situation through. How could you lose? How could you prevent that loss from happening? And if you do lose, how could you still be okay?

You can reduce the risk of a debilitating loss by using the full R.E.D.U.C.E. process. We have already seen how Stephanie avoided the big fear of losing too much money. Even if she has to hire a second editor, she can still clear $1,600. Stephanie's fear is reduced.

Next, I guided her to consider a vendor who can do print-on-demand, so Stephanie's first order was ten books for a small fee. In this way, she reduced her fear still further by selecting a small action.

Make [your] first action step so tiny and nonthreatening that you stop being afraid … If you want to lower your fear level, lower the danger level. – Barbara Sher

Now Stephanie can have a friend send an e-mail to a local editors' guild's list of members. This is a small step toward hiring her first editor.

When we lower the danger level, reduce fear, and take action, we create opportunities for success and feelings of fulfillment.

In talking with successful people, I have discovered that they have developed skills for dealing with rejection. In fact, many say that it is their ability to face and persist through rejection that has made the difference in creating their massive success. Successful people make sure that any fear of possible rejection does *not* stop them from making the next phone call and meeting the next person.

Just imagine: **What would you do if you had no fear?**

Grab a sheet of paper or your journal and write down your answer.

My client Marina wrote, "I would call the local college's illustration department and find a good student to illustrate the children's book I've written."

Your life will change when you experience this process: Every year I live a new year. I do new things. I move beyond fear. Remember …

Do the thing we fear, and death of fear is certain.

– Ralph Waldo Emerson

Create an environment in which you can rehearse. If you fear public speaking, join Toastmasters. Do something proactive. For example, the popular comedian Don Rickles discovered his comedy act by dealing with hecklers.

A man of courage is also full of faith. - Marcus Tullius Cicero

Take a step forward. You will lift your spirits and the spirits of those around you.

There is no duty we so underrate as the duty of being happy. By being happy we sow anonymous benefits upon the world.

– Robert Louis Stevenson

We discover that we can enjoy happy times when we learn to move beyond fear. We do not let the fear of loss control us. We remember to think the situation through.

- Identify how to prevent a loss.
- Plan how we can recover if a loss occurs.

Unleash Yourself from Social Pressures
Handle social pressures

Stephanie wants the approval of other authors in her industry. She also wants to position herself for greater success. A solution is for Stephanie to hire two editors on purpose. She then has double the possibility of getting her work to rise to the level of excellence.

The greatest communicators realize that fear subsides when you devote yourself to the process and focus in the moment.

The way you overcome shyness is to become so wrapped up in something that you forget to be afraid. – Lady Bird Johnson

The point here is that Stephanie can immerse herself in the process of refining her book's text. She can view the corrections noted by the first editor, make revisions, and improve the quality of her book. Then she can give her revised draft to a second editor, the "last-eyes editor."

The most productive people in any field realize that in order to improve, you need to practice your craft. It is likely that Stephanie's next book will be better than her current book. We learn by doing.

We can also learn to deal with criticism of our earliest work. Some people feel social pressure because they fear that they cannot recover from the criticism of their early work.

I worked with a client, a filmmaker, who found that someone had taken excerpts from her first film and placed them on YouTube.com. She developed her own answers to criticism:

- "Did you laugh?"
- "Works for some; doesn't work for others."
- "That was at the beginning of my career."
- "That's a part of my body of work."

Just knowing how she would be able to respond to any criticism lowered my client's fear level. With less fear, she was free to devote her energy to her current work. Do you see how being prepared for criticism can free up your personal energy?

Cover the Cost
Handle perceived cost

"How much does it cost?" Some salespeople dread this question. If the perceived cost of any project is too high, a person is unlikely to take action. However, when you want to be at your best, you must uncover the real cost of inaction.

The real cost of inaction can be the loss of an opportunity. Or it can be the pain of remaining stuck in a rut. Not taking action can create stagnation. That is the real cost of inaction. The real cost hurts. Imagine being stuck in a dead-end job, or being stuck in your own small business and barely hanging on. Now that we know the real cost of inaction, we can carefully and strategically plan our next move.

If a problem can be solved with money, it is no longer a problem. It is an expense. – Harvey Mackay

This is how Stephanie steps up, reduces her risk and takes action: when she thinks through her options and runs the numbers, she discovers that she can handle an additional cost if it proves necessary. As we saw earlier, if she must hire a second editor to make up for the first editor's mistakes, she will have invested $1,400—and she can still clear $1,600. This realization makes it easier for Stephanie to take action.

Engage in Rehearsal
Fear helps us when we use it as a springboard for preparation and as energy for heightened senses.

What is a prime cure for nervousness? Rehearsal. After years of speaking to audiences, I still get occasional pre-speech jitters. My solution? Whenever I have a driver to take me to a speaking engagement, I rehearse in the car.

It is no use saying, 'We are doing our best.' You have got to succeed in doing what is necessary. – Winston Churchill

The necessary thing is to move forward. Taking action is

necessary. Rehearsing is necessary. Taking action does not make us immune to mistakes, but using the R.E.D.U.C.E. process makes it possible to avoid much damage.

Strive not to be a success, but rather to be of value.
– Albert Einstein

When you focus on giving value, you can let go of the fear that you're not perfect.

Part II, Section 3
Power Thought / Physiology Process
(The Three-Fs)

A man who is afraid will do anything. – Jawaharlal Nehru

We can use this insight. We can take our fear and convert it into empowering energy by using the Three-Fs process:

Find your fear –> Flip it –> Forward It.

See the process below and fill in your own answers per the examples on the next page.

The idea of "relaxing into" tells us that there are some things that we cannot solve with action. For example, to recover from the stress and strain of a hectic day, we actually need to disengage from our schedule of rushing around and just relax. So sometimes "what I can do" becomes simply to take six minutes for quiet time.

When I'm on a train, I set my timer for six minutes. I do some deep breathing and repeat a relaxing phrase in my mind. This brightens my day.

The Three-Fs Process
Questions:
(Find It) What are you afraid of?

46

(Flip It) What do you really want?

(Forward It) What can you do? What can you relax into?

Example:

(Find It) "I'm afraid of inadequate funds to support my spouse and me in retirement."

(Flip It) "I want an abundance of funds for retirement."

(Forward It) "Make a list of my talents. Look into how I can use these talents on a part-time basis and ..."

Judge each day not by the harvest you reap, but by the seeds you plant. – Robert Louis Stevenson

By having a daily six-minute quiet time, you plant seeds of success. Similarly, you plant seeds by using the Three-Fs process to transform your experience of fear into a sense of power.

Now I'll share a personal example to show you the Three-Fs process in action. My sweetheart likes roller-coasters. Over the years, I found myself wanting to avoid being knocked about by this kind of thrill ride. Let's see how this looks.

The Three-Fs Process

Find It –> Flip It –> Forward It

What are you afraid of ?

Adding discomfort to my day by being knocked about by a thrill ride.

What do you really want?

To enjoy time with my sweetheart, doing what she likes to do.

What can you do? What can you relax into?

This brought me to the point of discovering what I could do to forward it—to move forward from fear into fulfillment.

Fortunately, I saw a documentary about roller-coasters. I

learned that many roller-coaster fans actually enjoy the queasy experience of zero gravity as the roller-coaster goes over the peaks on the ride. They call that moment "airtime."

I resolved to take the empowering word "airtime" with me on the next roller-coaster ride with my sweetheart. When we went through the zero-gravity times, I told myself, "This is airtime. People like this." And something amazing happened: I got a whole new interpretation of the thrill ride experience.

Now I have my favorite roller-coasters at Walt Disney World: Rock 'n' Roller Coaster and Expedition Everest. I also appreciate Top Gun at Great America in California. By having an empowering thought, I changed my experience of the event.

Let's notice that the Power Thought/Physiology Process (Three-Fs) begins with a question. In response to this question, you have a thought. Effective thoughts actually change your physiology in a way that benefits your life.

You are today where your thoughts have brought you; you will be tomorrow where your thoughts take you. – James Allen

Part III
How to Help People Feel at Ease
and to Want to Say "Yes!" to You

When I was in Walt Disney World, I wanted to get something done that was different and against the stated policy. To gain people's cooperation, I made sure to tune in to their language.

At a fantasy photo concession, I wanted a photo in which my friend and I looked like we were flying, but Disney World policy indicated that photos needed to show the customer performing a skydiving motion. I said to the person taking photos, "This photo is a fantasy anyway. Have us flying, just like Peter Pan."

My friend had whispered in my ear, "Just like Superman." But as part of my strategy, I avoided saying anything about Superman (a Warner Bros/DC Comics character). By using the language of Disney, thereby making it easy for them to honor my unusual request, I gained agreement to my suggestion.

We will use the W.I.N.–T.H.E.–P.R.I.Z.E. process:

W – Walk up the chain of command
I - Impress the person that you're staying
N – Nudge politely
T – Tune in to language
H – Hone your approach
E – Establish your credibility
P – Persist
R – Record notes
I— Itemize "this or that"
Z – Zero in on de-escalating
E – Encounter the reputable

Walk Up the Chain of Command

At the bottom of the chain of command of any organization, you have clerks, whose role is only to respond to stated policies. To get action that is beyond the organization's policy, you need to go up the chain of command. Politely ask, "Please connect me with your supervisor." If the clerk says, "I'm sorry. That person is not in today," you can respond, "Please pass me to someone on the same level as your supervisor or above," or, "That's not going to get me satisfaction today."

To get what you want, you may need to stretch. This reminds me of the experience of Jack Canfield, bestselling coauthor of the *Chicken Soup for the Soul* series. He began giving seminars many years ago, and he was having some financial trouble. He went to another speaker and asked, "How do you get $800 a day?" This was a large sum in those days.

"I ask for it," the speaker replied.

Jack described his clenched feelings as he tried to get the words out the next time he was asked, "What is your fee?" He was in the clutch of fear. Finally, he managed to say, "Ughhhh—$800 a day."

"Okay," the person replied. In that moment, Jack became an $800-per-day speaker. Now he makes $35–70,000 per keynote address.

Jack was surprised that the person said "okay" so readily. That same outcome often happens when we gently press for what we want.

Principle: Move up the chain of command to interact with one who has the authority to solve the problem.

Power Question: What words feel better for you to use when you ask to talk with someone in authority?

Impress the Person that You're Staying

Do what you feel in your heart to be right—for you'll be criticized anyway. – Eleanor Roosevelt

Make sure that your words and tone impress the person that you are *not* going away. You can say, "So, what does your firm do to take care of good customers who have been inconvenienced?" You can follow up with, "Perhaps I need to talk with your supervisor or someone higher up to get satisfaction today." In addition to making it clear that you will not give up, you must stay polite. If you lose your temper, the person can "write you off." Instead, by politely but firmly holding your ground, you will get help towards a solution.

Principle: You can gain a solution by impressing the person that you will stay, and by politely requiring satisfaction.

Power Question: Who will help you rehearse polite but firm statements?

Nudge Politely

A hotel refused to let people check into their rooms before three in the afternoon. I said, "You have two guests who have been awake for 48 hours. Either we're going to have to fall asleep in the first aid section, or you can provide the service that (name of the hotel firm) is so famous for and find us another room. Do you need to talk with your manager about this?" Within three minutes, the room was found.

My use of the phrase "the service that (name of the hotel firm) is so famous for" was a form of verbal aikido. Aikido is a martial art in which you use your opponent's force against him. Basically, you guide the opponent in the direction he is already going. The use of verbal aikido ties in with the principle, "nudge politely."

Non-resistance, non-judgment, and non-attachment are the three aspects of true enlightenment. – Eckhart Tolle

The effective person avoids creating resistance in the one she's dealing with. If you get angry or insult the person or company, you hurt yourself by creating resistance. As in aikido, it is better to gently but firmly guide the person towards the outcome you prefer.

Principle: As in aikido, it often helps to nudge a person in the direction in which you want him or her to go.

Power Question: How can you clearly and politely

communicate what you want?

Tune in to Language

Have you noticed that organizations have buzzwords? When you use them, you create the feeling that, "Yes, we're in this together."

Some doctors use language to keep a distance from their patients. Their language shows, "We're in the know, and you're not," or "We're in the 'in group.' "

Using the appropriate language can help you gain what you want. Study the language of the profession of the person you want to influence. Use his or her language to develop a rapport.

In my book *Nothing Can Stop You This Year!* I introduce my concept, the Ease-Through™. Many people try to push their point and encounter resistance. The pusher tries harder, and the other person resists harder. The pusher wants a breakthrough, like a karate punch to a board.

With the Ease-Through, you just remove the board. This is the power of effective language. Avoid saying, "I want a refund!" Ask instead, "So, how does Acme Company keep loyal customers happy?"

Nothing is softer or more flexible than water, yet nothing can resist it. – Lao-tzu

Principle: Use the other person's language to develop a rapport with him or her.

Power Question: What sources of information can you go to, such as a Google Search, before your meeting so that you can be prepared to speak in the other person's language (use their buzzwords)?

Hone Your Approach

How can you be at your best when you need to influence

someone? Dictionary.com defines *hone* as "to make more acute or effective; improve; perfect: to hone one's skills."

A powerful way to hone any skill is to have winning experiences. A workshop or a private coaching session is an ideal place for this to occur. For the clients I coach, I invite them to send me 10 specific questions before the coaching session. Then we focus on their specific areas of concern.

In my workshops, I have coached participants in how to have a vocal tone that is firm and friendly. A friendly, firm approach is to have a pleasant tone and repeat gently, "Thanks for your efforts on this. And we still need to get me satisfaction today. Who has the power to help keep your loyal customer happy about this situation?"

At the center of your being you have the answer; you know who you are and you know what you want. – Lao-tzu

To get to the quiet center of our being, many of us take deep calming breaths, pray or meditate before calling or seeing another person for a vital conversation.

To the mind that is still, the whole universe surrenders.

– Lao-tzu

To have a friendly, firm approach, you need to know your own natural rhythms and take care of yourself. When you talk with someone, you need to have a reserve of patience and calm energy. For example, Sylvester "Sly" Stallone, actor and screenwriter of *Rocky*, started out and discovered his own creative rhythms. Sly said, "In New York, I wrote from midnight to the morning I wrote my most nihilistic material. I went through my [Edgar Allen] Poe period."

On the other hand, Sly took a different approach to the screenplay for *Rocky*. He said, "To write *Rocky*, I wrote early in the morning. I was writing from 6:00 in the morning until 12 noon … I use a big pencil because at the end of six hours you're writing like this [holding the pencil in his fist] … If I had a problem writing, I told my subconscious mind, I want you to solve it by morning."

We notice that Sly Stallone used all his resources, including his subconscious mind. As a sidenote, Sly said, "Redemption is one of my themes. I never met anyone who didn't want a second chance." He took a big chance when he added 41 pounds to play a washed-out sheriff in Copland, and he also took a big pay cut for the role, from the $20 million he received for *Daylight* to $60,000. He emphasized, "In the great quest of self-satisfaction ... I would always go to the unsafe zone ... I believe in taking risks—every time out." Sly's performance as the sheriff in *Copland* was considered excellent by many critics and audience members.

To get people to want to say "yes" to you, learn to ask gentle questions. Using gentle questions is one of the best parts of a positive, effective approach. Author Gene Bedell wrote about these powerful questions:

1. Yes, I understand those are your company's needs. But what are you looking for? What's most important to you personally?

2. Let's project into the future. What do you visualize as the ideal outcome? How would things work if you could write the script and everything went as you'd like it to go?

3. It would help me understand what the best outcome in the future would be if you'd describe what you don't like about the current (or past) situation. From a personal standpoint, what change would you like to see?

4. I'm sure you're looking at other options. What do you personally like about the best options you've seen so far?

Gene Bedell emphasizes that people buy something to fulfill their personal needs. You learn how to persuade a person when you know details about her. Gentle questions open the door.

Principle: Hone your approach by taking a good look at how you interpret what happens. Then find and practice methods to empower yourself.

Power Questions: How can you adapt to what is going on so that you recover from what bothers you? How can you re-interpret what is going on so that you can approach the situation calmly? How can you lower your own stress levels?

Establish Your Credibility

You can't follow someone who isn't credible, who doesn't truly believe in what they're doing—and how they're doing it.

– Gayle Hamilton (Pacific Gas & Electric)

How do you get better treatment from a clerk? People treat a caller better when he or she has some social standing. On only two occasions, I have found it necessary to say, "I'm a national speaker who talks with corporations on customer service. I write for a number of blogs and I would prefer to continue my good impression of your firm. So how can we handle this detail?"

Sometimes, it helps if you demonstrate that you have influence. The ability to influence others (especially those who can have an impact on the company's bottom line) can be an important factor in credibility.

An interviewer asked me, "But if you say that you write for a number of newsletters, aren't you bullying the person you're talking to?"

"I'm glad you asked me this," I replied. "It reminds me of my work with a number of clients. It helps to know and to feel in your bones the *difference* between being assertive and being aggressive. I helped one particular woman become assertive. When her parents were having difficulty getting a fair amount from an insurance company to repair their car, she learned to say, 'That's not working for us. Can you do better than that?' This statement is assertive. You notice that it is polite but firm." A friend told me, "In this time of the Internet, you can create instant credibility. In one day you could start your own e-newsletter and send it to your friends. Then you could say something like, 'I write for a publication called The Customer Service Journal."

Remember, if you have some influence with people who are important to the company you're dealing with, you may get the treatment and results you want. (Having a blog helps. My blog YourBodySoulandProsperity.com reaches visitors from 69 countries.)

Principle: Establish your credibility.

Power Question: How can you express your credentials in a way that gets the person concerned about what you might report?

Persist

Being deeply loved by someone gives you strength; loving someone deeply gives you courage. – Lao-tzu

This quote identifies a source that many of us can use to have the strength to persist.

There is one way to get what you want: persist. When you are willing to go up the chain of command to the CEO, you are strong. You will get some form of satisfaction. Why? Because as you go up the chain of command, you will encounter the vice president, for example, who feels that her time is valuable. She wants the situation resolved quickly so she can return to leading her department. Also, the higher up you go, the more power the person has to override any stated policy.

Principle: Persist. There is no substitute.

Power Question: How can you persist? Would it help if

you use a phone call, e-mail, a letter, contact a television consumer advocate … ?

Record Notes

How can you save $100,000 on a significant deal? Write notes for each important conversation. Author Roger Dawson knows someone who saved $100,000 when he asked the other person to check his notes. The person did not have thorough notes, and Roger Dawson's friend prevailed.

All problems become smaller if you don't dodge them, but confront them. – William F. Halsey

We need to confront any hesitation we may have to writing notes. The benefit of recording notes far outweighs any discomfort.

When you have good notes, you can often get your way because the other person may have failed to take any notes. You can say, "Would you check your notes? According to my notes of January 22nd, at 12:45 p.m. we discussed X and Y and resolved to do Z."

Often upon closing a transaction, I request that a memo be e-mailed to my office to confirm the solution.

Principle: Record notes of each interaction with a company's personnel.

Power Question: What will you use (a notebook, binder, computer file, or contact management program) to record your notes?

Itemize "This or That"

How can you influence a person to give an answer in your favor? Provide a "this or that" solution.

For example, you could say, "It would help me feel better if your company provided me with a refund or a coupon for this …"

Make it easier for the person to say "yes." Give her a

choice between two specific options, both of which would satisfy you.

It is only with the heart that one can see rightly, what is essential is invisible to the eye. – Antoine De Saint Exupéry

Antoine's comment reminds us that we need to get to the heart of the matter. What do you really want? And how can you express that as an easy "this or that" solution?

Principle: Make it easier to get a "yes" by providing two options.

Power Question: How can you phrase two options that make it easier for the person to say "yes" than "no"?

Zero in on De-Escalating

What can save you time and tension? Use de-escalating language. At the beginning of your transaction, speak gently. For example, some years ago I helped a family member deal with a company. I said to the clerk, "Oh, we just need a little adjustment here, only 20 dollars." The magic de-escalating word was adjustment. I did not say, "I want my family member's money back." I avoided the phrase, "Give me a refund!"

Contributing to other people's happiness provides us with meaning and pleasure … an unhappy person is less likely to be benevolent. – Tal Ben-Shahar

If you use intense or escalating language, you are likely to make a person unhappy. When you use de-escalating language, you contribute to his or her well-being. You find a way to create cooperation. You help the person to do a good job. In the spirit of cooperation, you gently suggest solutions—which benefit you.

Principle: Begin by using de-escalating language.

Power Question: How can you re-phrase comments in ways that make the other person feel at ease?

Encounter the Reputable

It's better to hang out with people better than you. Pick out associates whose behavior is better than yours, and you'll drift in that direction. – Warren Buffet

When you work with established, reputable firms that build their business on repeat customers and referrals, you will get satisfaction. However, let's face it together: there are some firms that truly do not care. Stay away from them.

Over the years, I have appreciated the excellent customer service of Franklin-Covey (makers of day planners) and Walt Disney Resorts. Both companies train their employees in excellent customer service.

The Disney organization's training program is entitled Traditions, to emphasize the core value of service. Disney employees are trained to call customers *guests.* For example, on the Disney Cruise that my sweetheart and I enjoyed, many details were orchestrated to delight us. Even the way the ship's cabin was decorated provided charming surprises. The artistry included towels that were formed into cute, attractive animals.

When I returned and spoke to my next audience, my one-word comment about the Disney Cruise was, "Woooooow!"

Principle: Encounter the reputable firms that build their business on repeat customers and referrals.

Power Questions: How can you get information about a company before you purchase its product or service? Will you study blogs? Visit consumer-advocate Web sites?

Part IV
How Great Communicators
Overcome the #1 Obstacle to Happiness

What is the number one obstacle to happiness? I will answer this question in a moment.

First, here's a crucial detail: Please know that a profound truth may often be disguised as something that sounds simple. You may have a reaction like, "Oh, I've heard that before." But the essential question is: Have you done anything with that knowledge?

There's an old phrase: "To know and not to do is not to know." So, what is the number one obstacle to happiness? *It is not to be in this moment, now.*

What does that mean? If you're worrying about the future or feeling guilty over the past, you are *not* in this moment.

How do you get into this moment? Gratitude.

For example, I am grateful for the computer into which I'm typing these words. I'm grateful that you are reading this book. I am grateful that I have a purpose and dreams, and that I am committed to them.

What does this number one obstacle to happiness have to do with the secrets of the greatest communicators?

The answer is—everything.

If you're not focused in the moment, your listener can sense that you're distracted. She might assume that you do not care about her.

The way we communicate with others and with ourselves ultimately determines the quality of our lives. – Tony Robbins

How do we communicate powerfully with ourselves? We carefully choose the questions we ask ourselves.

If you're worrying, "How am I doing?" the audience can

sense that preoccupation. Switch to, "How can I serve *you? How are you* doing?"

The solution is to bring yourself back to the present moment. This became clear to me one year when I injured my back. The pain was so bad that I grunted involuntarily in agony a number of times. A concerned friend asked me, "How are you doing?"

I replied, "Making the most of this moment." This was a truthful reply. The pain in my back varied from moment to moment. When I rose from a chair, I would feel a disabling, stabbing pain in my lumbar area. But when I walked, the pain was less.

One powerful way to focus on the moment is to silently repeat, "Be in the moment."

I don't believe people are looking for the meaning of life as much as they are looking for the experience of being alive.

– Joseph Campbell

Immerse yourself in this moment. Enjoy what is here now.

I never lose sight of the fact that just being is fun.

– Katherine Hepburn

Learn to get into this moment. Use a phrase like *Be here now* to help you let go of distracting thoughts.

A man is rich in proportion to the number of things he can afford to leave alone. – Henry David Thoreau

Henry's quote reminds us that we may need to let go of a particular thought in order to immerse ourselves in the present moment.

Get into this moment. Say to yourself, "I am grateful for … " People who are grateful radiate charisma and good will. They are fun to be around.

My clients report that they tell themselves:

- I am grateful to be talking with Janet now.

- I am grateful for this job.
- I am grateful for this opportunity to speak to this audience.

The quickest, easiest way to connect with God is to express your gratitude. – M.J. Ryan

Expressing gratitude can restore a relationship. At one point, my father was upset with me. He would not come to the telephone when I called my parents' home. Prior to this, he had stopped using e-mail. So I found a different way to connect. I sent him a happy-looking card that depicted Kermit the Frog playing the banjo. I wrote:

Dad,

Happy today. Thank you for holding me to high standards. This has made my life better.

Love, Tom

This heartfelt message helped my father feel better. Soon we were talking on the phone and meeting again in person.

Sometimes it takes extra effort to connect with gratitude. Some of us say, "How can I be grateful? My brother has just died." The process of grief can overwhelm our perception.

While I was writing this book, a close friend (like a brother) died. I found that I didn't know from moment to moment whether I would choke up with grief or smile while remembering my friend's loving kindness and sense of humor. There were moments when I felt grateful for the opportunities to share time with him before he died.

In class, I told my graduate students the truth about my sadness over my dear friend's death. I could see in their faces that many of them had gone through a similar grieving time. This strengthened our connection. I said, "I may lose my voice for 30 seconds. But that's okay ... we'll keep flowing forward."

It is natural—you need to smile to your sorrow because you are more than your sorrow. – Thich Nhat Hanh

So even while I was experiencing intense grief, I flowed with each moment.

We do not remember days, we remember moments.
– Cesare Pavese

During this time of grief for my friend, I learned to flow with my feelings. And after a time of tears, I felt drawn to uplifting thoughts and experiences, such as soothing music.

Follow your bliss, and doors will open for you that you never knew existed. – Joseph Campbell

This is such a hopeful idea! I have seen it come true many times in my life. I wrote a screenplay that impressed the California Motion Picture Commissioner, and three years later he secured (at no cost) an American Eagle airplane and an airport runway for a feature film I was directing. I followed my bliss, and amazing and unexpected doors opened for me.

Happiness and Goals

Tal Ben-Shahar, author of *Happier* (the source material for Harvard University's most popular course) wrote, "The proper role of goals is to liberate us, so we can enjoy the here and now … Happiness is the overall experience of pleasure and meaning."

Now let's look at happiness in the context of big success.

Jaws is something that I'll never forget. It is something that I don't want to repeat … The experience of making Jaws was horrendous for me … I am completely grateful to the audience embracing the movie and the movie being such a phenomenon—which basically gave me what I had always dreamed about—which was (a) being a movie director and (b) having final cut. And Jaws gave me freedom. – Steven Spielberg

Be happy in the here and now. Focus on the process. Each

day has ups and downs. Celebrate each small victory.

I am an extraordinarily lucky person, doing what I love best in the world. I'm sure that I will always be a writer. It was wonderful enough just to be published. The greatest reward is the enthusiasm of the readers. – J.K. Rowling

From this quote, we see that J.K. Rowling, the fabulously wealthy author of the *Harry Potter* books, knows that she simply loves writing!

Keep a gratitude journal. Every night, list five things that happened this day that you are grateful for. What it will begin to do is change your perspective of your day and your life ... Be thankful for what you have ... If you can learn to focus on what you have, you will always see that the universe is abundant; you will have more. If you concentrate on what you don't have, you will never have enough. – Oprah Winfrey

I guide my clients and audiences to use a **Daily Journal of Victories and Blessings.** (A victory is what you accomplish; a blessing is something pleasant like a surprise phone call with a friend.)

One day, Bob Greene, Oprah's trainer, asked her, "When was the last time you experienced joy?" Oprah thought for a while and replied that it had been seven years. This question inspired her to modify her TV show (at the time) and take it to a higher level, to "help people lead better, more meaningful lives."

Here's a secret: Find ways to experience some joy each day. My clients have noted their joyful moments:
- Listening to music that reminds me of a fun concert I attended
- Talking with my spouse
- Going for a walk
- Writing my novel for a half-hour as soon as I get home from work

With my audiences, I emphasize, "Make it a game you can win." It's up to you. You can schedule some moments every day to devote to something that brings you joy, comfort, meaning or peace. I travel a lot, and I find that even devoting three minutes to quiet time on a train brightens my whole day.

Brighten your day. Raise your morale so that you radiate good will. Please write "Quiet time," or "15 minutes painting my picture," or something that brings you joyful moments into your day planner.

Principle: Focus on this moment—now.

Power Question: How can you use a certain phrase to remind you to return to the present moment? (Example: "I am grateful to be talking with Janet now.")

Part V
Secrets to Increase Your Income & Prosperity

At one point, an interviewer asked me, "What are some secrets of making money?" I replied that I have personally used a set of principles that I created for my clients and myself.

(Communication around financial concerns is important. Also, we need to communicate effectively with ourselves.)

I'm so concerned about misinformation in general use that I streamlined the principles into the T.R.U.T.H. process for making money.

T – Transform to "Yes."

R – Run in better races.

U – Untangle from the money-for-time trade.

T – Take on risk.

H – Hone your persuasion skills.

A great source of feeling calm in turbulent financial times is to have hope. See which of the T.R.U.T.H. process methods seize your attention and then make an action plan. In this way you will have the hope you need to rise out of any financial rut.

As you take baby steps forward, you will begin to feel more hopeful.

Action is the antidote to despair. - Joan Baez

Transform to "Yes"

Have you noticed that people often have an automatic "no" response to new ideas or new actions? When some new opportunity to earn money comes along, many of us find that "no" rises up. "No, I won't be good enough." "No, they'll reject me and that will feel bad."

Instead, I invite you to transform that "no" to a big "Yes."

• "Yes, I'm going to give this a chance."

• "Yes, I can handle a possible rejection. Instead, I'll call it 'we didn't have a match.'"

As a teenager, I began my work life at a fast food restaurant making minimum wage. I was 15 years old and I washed everything, including floors, windows and toilets. The first time I earned $400 an hour, I stepped significantly out of my comfort zone. I earned that $400 modeling for an advertisement for a software company.

I was afraid during that photo shoot. Why? When I walked into the building, the photographer said, "You were born in the U.S., weren't you?" At that point my jangled nerves felt like I wanted to escape out a window. Apparently, I was going to be rejected (even though he had seen my actor photo) and I would lose the money I had paid to travel to the site of the photoshoot.

I went into action and applied my actor's training: To

make the photo function, I placed my hands together in a reverent manner like I had seen Asian monks do. The photographer took a photo of my head and shoulders. He said, "That's better." Evidently my posture had changed from the hard-charging energy that I usually walked around with. I was playing the role of someone raised in an Asian country — that was the assessment of the photographer.

Here is an important part of Transform to "Yes": **Step out of your comfort zone and make the best of a situation.**

I remember the first time that I made thousands of dollars through the Internet. I was seized with an idea. At the time I was on a train en route to teaching a graduate level class. I took quick notes. Upon arriving, I walked quickly to the university. I went into a side room and quickly typed out two thousand words on my laptop. My point here is that **I said "Yes!" to the idea.** I took action and ultimately completed writing a new e-book. People in 15 countries purchased that e-book (then book) through the Internet. The title is: *Darkest Secrets of Persuasion and Seduction Masters: How to Protect Yourself and Turn the Power to Good.*

When I wrote the first two thousand words of the e-book, I had no idea if what I wrote would work. But I had another "Yes" response.

"Yes, it's all good practice. I'll get better as a writer."

"Yes, I can probably adapt this writing to something else in the future."

Run in Better Races
Years ago I was feeling overwhelmed. I told my sweetheart, "I'm like a racehorse."

"Run in better races," she replied, encouraging me to be more selective.

Good point. This led to my idea: *I need to be in an area*

where a big payday is possible.

This proved to be true the first time I earned $1,000 in one hour. At the time I was earning $14 an hour as a marketing assistant.

My question was: *Is there something I can do that comes easy to me, but is hard for other people?*

Write down your own possible answers to this question, which I will repeat: Is there something I can do that comes easy to me, but is hard for other people?

I knew I could study, synthesize information, and convey it in an entertaining way.

Acclaimed Television Host Johnny Carson said, "People will pay more to be entertained than to be educated." So I earned $1000 in one hour by speaking to a group on a topic which I had never presented before. (This was so many years ago.)

An interviewer commented, "It sounds like it takes chutzpah and courage to try new things and put yourself at risk."

Often, one needs to act with courage. My audiences like my phrase, **Courage is easier when I'm prepared.** The point is that I prepare every day for my next speech, interview or book that I write. In recent years, I have read 74 books per year. I prepare by keeping up with my fields of interest.

How does one get into a better race?

It's about your skills in building relationships. And the essence of effective networking (for jobs and more) is building good relationships. So often opportunities that I have enjoyed have come from building business and personal relationships. Years ago, my first opportunity to be marketed by a speaker bureau at the $5,000 level came from years of building a relationship with the bureau's team members. This is how you get in a better race. You are friendly, trustworthy and helpful in all your dealings with people. Then people bring you opportunities.

The truth about dealing with a financial crisis

Let me tell you about someone I truly admire. Linda had trained as a graphic designer for the hi-tech industry. But when the Silicon Valley Dot-Com Bubble burst, she went through some pain and had to shift gears. Through the years she gained training in a number of fields so that she has multiple ways to bring value to the marketplace. Currently she is one of my editors. She is also a personal chef, author and weight loss counselor. Formerly she was a hair stylist and hair salon owner. Let's learn from Linda's example: Make sure that you can earn money in many ways. **This is called having multiple streams of income.** I invite you to follow Linda's example and look for possibilities to use your hidden talents and gain new training for when a crisis arrives.

An interviewer asked: "Does a person need to be assertive?"

It depends on the situation. **Would you like to know four sentences that meant $321,043 to me?**

After I gave a speech, an audience member walked up to me and said, "You should speak for ___ Company." I replied, "Thank you. Who do I talk with? [He told me.] Oh, you have your cell phone? How about we leave her a message now?" Those were the four sentences. The person immediately left a voicemail message and I ultimately closed the deal (that resulted in a number of presentations).

The point here is that I needed to be assertive. First I needed to notice if I had enough rapport with the person who praised me and said, "You should speak for ___ Company." Also, the reason why the four sentences were important is because the man who gave me the compliment was at a peak in his emotional approval of my speaking. That's the reason I wanted him to immediately leave a voicemail message. I knew his enthusiasm would appear on that message.

Untangle from the Money-for-Time Trade

Many of us are caught in a real trap: Trading one hour of our time for a certain amount of money. Even when I set my hourly rate higher and higher, I realized that there was an upper limit on an hourly wage. But if I could write books … I would do the work once and get paid again and again.

For example, I wrote material for actors and was paid multiple times, including:

- Fees paid for teaching classes.
- Fees paid by students at the classes who chose to purchase the workbook at a cost of $25 each.
- Fees paid in recent years by people who purchased the same material as a book entitled *Darkest Secrets of the Film and Television Industry Every Actor Should Know: A Film Director and Actor Reveals Secrets for Your Acting, Auditions, Movie Roles, and Self-Promotion.*

Another example: Author Joel Osteen is not in the trap of trading time for money. Joel reportedly earned a $13 million advance fee for his second book. As a pastor he speaks to his in-person congregation of around 40,000 people each Sunday. And millions more view his television broadcasts. As I mentioned earlier: You need to be in an area where a big payday is possible. Joel lives this secret.

An interviewer commented: "Well, that's good for Joel. He has a whole team. His father had built the congregation up to 8,000 people before Joel Osteen took over."

Excellent points! This reminds us that there are no self-made millionaires. Everyone rises to a higher level with the cooperation, help, and guidance of others.

Five ways to stop trading time for money
Write something

If you have some writing talent and you enjoy writing to some measure, consider writing a book, a novel, a screenplay, an audio program or graphic novel. With writing, a secret is to continually make progress. If you write an article, the material can later appear in an audio program, speech or book. I write some material every day. Some of my clients choose self-publishing and sell their material on the Internet; and other clients go the traditional route of agents and getting a book deal with a major publisher.

This is an "and" universe; that is, you can do one thing and another. A writer can pursue both routes. Some people hesitate because they do not feel like an expert. I alert my clients to the empowering idea that *an expert is someone who has devised a system that people like and use.* To become an expert may be a lower hurdle than many of us think. Many people start with a personal problem, learn how to solve it, and then train others to solve that problem.

Invent something

Some of us remember the Pet Rock, which was merely a rock with brilliantly witty packaging. Gary Dahl, the man with the idea, offered his graphic designer $50,000 to sell his share of the project. So Gary went on to take the risks and gain the benefits solo. Soon Gary earned $1 million with the Pet Rock.

To find your inspiration, you might read books or watch

television shows like "American Inventor." For example, viewers were enthralled when they saw a fireman, Gregg Chavez, propose an idea for a fire safety device called The Guardian Angel. Chavez described his Guardian Angel invention as, "A small, pressurized tank of water, disguised as a Christmas package that is placed under the Christmas tree and attached to a small hose leading to the top of the tree where a fusible link is disguised as an angel. The heat from a fire pops the link and water suppresses the fire."

Close real estate deals

As this is being written, a number of real estate agents express their concerns about how the real estate market has faltered. Let's realize that the real estate business, like a number of other industries, cycles back. For example, a friend recently told me that his real estate agent made $6,000 on the sale of a home. When I mentioned this in an interview, the host said, "Wait a minute. That still sounds like trading time for money." I replied, "I see your point. And, we realize that once a real estate agent acquires the knowledge for closing deals, she can be working on multiple deals at the same time. A number of effective real estate agents have an assistant that does much of the routine office work. This is all about multiplying one's ability to earn large sums in less time. This process is still different from making a set fee of $20 per hour or even $300 per hour."

Sell through the Internet

Millions of people sell items through eBay. Others sell information-related products. For example, my friend author David Barron teamed up with another author (with a large e-subscribers list). David had written and put together a system that guides people to become powerful influencers, and David's share of the profits was $6,000! I have coached clients on how to interview top people in a field, write an article and place it on Web sites. This is how you begin relationships with other authors that can lead to joint, mutually beneficial ventures.

Author and Internet entrepreneur Randy Gage mentions these popular topics that can be written about and sold as an expert's opinion on the Internet: marketing strategies, home-based business, health and wellness, weight loss, sales, crafts, art, wealth building, spiritual enlightenment, finding good employees, relationships, Web site design, gardening, raising a family, nutrition, travel and presentation skills. I would add: ways to live well on a small budget, humor and pets.

Team up

Some of my audience members say, "I'm not a writer." Don't let that stop you. Years ago, as a ghostwriter, I wrote a speech for a millionaire. And this millionaire had previously sold 1.4 million copies of a (probably ghostwritten) book. Sometimes my clients ask me, "How did you write and publish three books in one year?" I reply that I have a system:

- I write the material.
- I read it out loud to a team member. I revise the material as I hear the spoken words and watch my team member's responses.
- Then I have two editors (one in California and one in another state work on the material).

You do not need to be a writer. A client, Marcy, talks into an audio recorder. She has a nephew type up the material. Then she hands the material to a part-time college instructor for revision.

Teaming up is a powerful strategy. For example, I have produced ten audio programs that have all generated income. But I did not purchase a sound-editing program for my office computer. Why? Because it is more cost effective for me in terms of time and money to go to a veteran sound engineer. He can perform a refinement on the program in 20 seconds when it would take me 20 minutes (of frustration) to do the same function. He has devoted 17 years of his life to his craft of sound engineering and editing. I can walk into his studio, record my material, and step out with a completed master recording within hours! Also, my sound engineer gives me guidance on how I can improve the program as we edit it. This guidance raises the level of quality. Remember to team up.

Constantly prepare for the home run.

The major principle for gaining sudden profits is to constantly prepare for the home run. That is, on a daily basis, practice and prepare so that when you're in the game you can gain a big, life-improving result. Being in the game may occur when someone says, "You should speak for Acme Company" (an experience I mentioned earlier). Being in the game can also be when you're meeting a friend's sister at a party and it turns out that she needs an employee like you. By the way, use a number of methods of this section so that you feel calm when you're meeting people. A person who experiences some calm and some happiness each day is the person who radiates charisma. People offer charismatic individuals new opportunities. And remember that people tend to like others who listen to them. When you experience calm and some happiness each day, you have more energy to listen to new people you meet.

The point is: a number of successful people who seem to become an overnight success have been devoting effort over a number of years. They have been continually improving their craft. That is, they constantly prepare for the home run. For example, Jon Stewart (star of "The Daily Show" on Comedy Central) said, "I can't believe how lucky I have been already. And it's not in 'Aw, shucks' ... I have worked really hard. And I've tried to get better."

I learned something about success when bestselling author Richard Carlson told me his journey when we appeared on a radio show together. Richard said, *"Don't Sweat the Small Stuff* was my tenth book." Richard loved to write and he kept going through nine previous books, each with varying degrees of success.

Richard was perfecting his writing style with every book he wrote. In this way he was constantly preparing for the home run, which became his bestselling book *Don't Sweat the Small Stuff.* Soon, Richard had a bestselling series, including *Don't Sweat the Small Stuff in Love, Don't Sweat the Small Stuff with Money* and others.

Take on Risk

Earlier in this book, in *Reduce Risk,* I described the R.E.D.U.C.E. process. Here I want to emphasize that life does not only reward hard work. Big profits often result when someone takes on appropriate risk. A number of people shy away from appropriate risk. That's because they do not have a strategy for risk-taking. Please see *Part II, Section Two, Reduce Risk* for methods that can brighten your life.

I will do what others will not do, so in the future I can do what others cannot do. – Randy Gage

Hone Your Persuasion Skills

Later in this book, I discuss the P.E.R.S.U.A.D.E. process. Here I want to emphasize that we truly can open the floodgates of financial abundance when we learn and practice positive persuasion skills. My life changed when I learned that persuasion can have positive outcomes—when I start focusing on how I can benefit the listener.

Win-win or no deal. – Stephen R. Covey

Positive persuasion is about making sure that a transaction results in benefits for both people—a win-win result. True success is built on positive business and personal relationships. Learn the skills of positive persuasion and gain a whole new world of opportunities.

Comfort can be desirable, but opportunities are fun!

Principles: In order to do better financially, you need to stretch and take appropriate risks.

Power Question: Where or how can you get additional training so you can have multiple streams of income?

Part VI
Great Communicators Win with Job Interviews

"An election is a grand job interview," former President Bill Clinton said at a private luncheon I attended. "Have a 20-minute talk, a 15-minute one, and a one-minute talk. If you can't express it in one minute, you don't know why you want it."

When Bill Clinton gave his secrets of public speaking, I listened with rapt attention. He said, "The microphone is your friend. It enables everyone to relax. Relax, overcome fears and speak plainly. Strip things down to straight talk..."

President Clinton also said, "The mechanics of leadership

in any public endeavor is a team sport. It's very important to focus on teamwork. It is important to have people on your team that are different from you."

President Ronald Reagan has often been called the Great Communicator. In 1984, in their first televised presidential election debate, his opponent, Walter Mondale, put in an unexpectedly strong performance. Mondale questioned Reagan's age and capacity to endure the intense demands of the presidency.

But then in the next debate, on October 21, 1984, Reagan effectively neutralized the issue when he said, "I will not make age an issue of this campaign. I am not going to exploit for political purposes my opponent's youth and inexperience."

The media dropped the topic of age, and Ronald Reagan went on to gain the office of President of the United States.

We began this section with Bill Clinton's comment about an election campaign as a job interview. What we see from both former Presidents is the ability to make a warm, human connection.

Being heard and trusted depends on your ability to make a warm, human connection.

The Bottom Line About Job Interviews

In a new employee, employers want the following:

1. High productivity

2. Low maintenance (getting along well with team members, and more)

3. A "bargain" (top value without having to pay top dollar)

How do you help someone easily decide to hire you? Ask questions. This means inquire as to what they really want in a new employee. It takes some finesse to ask an appropriate question at an appropriate time.

To influence anyone to make a decision that is in your favor, you need to know what the person wants and how the person wants it. The crucial method is to uncover the interviewer's preferred input style.

We receive input all day long. There's some input we like, some we don't, and some we are indifferent to. But your new job is on the line here. So it is best to learn how to identify the interviewer's preferred input style.

First, be prepared for when the interviewer asks, "Do you have any questions?"

Consider this question: "What has to happen for you to know that a candidate is ideal for this position?"

We use the phrase "what has to happen" to discover the person's preferred input style. Her preferred input style is how she prefers to receive information. There are three primary input styles: visual, auditory, and kinesthetic (touch).

Preferred input style: The clue that identifies the input style

Visual: "I need to see some sample work."

Auditory: "I'd like to hear comments from your references."

Kinesthetic (touch): "We need to find out if you'd work smoothly with the other team members. The next step is for you to have interviews with team members."

About the person with the kinesthetic-input style

People who prefer kinesthetic input often say,

- It didn't feel right to me.
- That feels like a good fit.
- I'm just not comfortable with that detail.
- I hope your presentation went smoothly.

An interviewer asked me how these comments specifically offer the clue that the person prefers kinesthetic input. Note how each sentence deals with touch. We see key words, such as, "feel right," "good fit," "not comfortable," and "smoothly."

Each interviewer is a unique individual with a preferred input style. The good news is that when you listen carefully, you can often discover what the preferred input style is. Then you can supply the right information in an effective way. That's when you can be heard and be trusted.

Principle: Ask appropriate questions to discover what is really important to the person, so that he or she will decide in your favor.

Power Questions: Practice asking questions that can help you learn vital information during your job interview. Which words flow easily from your mouth? How can you modify a particular question so that you get the information you need and still feel at ease?

Prepare for Questions

Ever been hit in an interview by a question that knocked you for a loop? Imagine being prepared for some of the toughest questions. Prepare for the standard questions:

1. I see a gap in your resume. What were you doing then?
2. Why did you leave your last position?
3. What do you want to be doing in five years?
4. Describe your ideal job.
5. What are your weaknesses?

I guide my clients to prepare by having two anecdotes ready to answer each of these questions (for a total of six anecdotes):

- Tell me about yourself (your strengths)

- Tell me about your weaknesses
- What are you best known for? (your personal brand)

Facts go in our brains. Stories go in our hearts. – Sandra Bloch

People don't buy with their head but with their heart. The heart is closer to the wallet than the head. – Mark Victor Hansen

The weaknesses question in particular gets job applicants in trouble. In the past, some misguided advice stated, "Cleverly say things to make the weakness actually sound like a hidden strength." Stop! Interviewers can see through that antiquated tactic.

Avoid the phony answer. A better approach is to say something such as, "In the past, I tended to be overly focused on details. To counter that tendency, I took a course in project management. In that workshop, I had an experience in which I used the 80/20 Principle to set priorities. Now I continue to practice what I learned by having a note posted on my day planner page that reads '80/20'."

Know your tendencies and compensate for them.

– Tom Marcoux

You can't expect to win unless you know why you lose.

– Benjamin Lipson

At a luncheon I attended, Bill Clinton was asked a tough question about his mistakes during his presidency. He replied that one of his mistakes was answering all the allegations of the Whitewater scandal. "I worried about this for about two years. [But then I realized] what you know is from the two minutes on the evening news. If I answered something about Whitewater, you would think I wasn't doing my job [about education, the environment and more]." Subsequently, Clinton made sure that the television sound bites were about something that was of value to his administration.

Bill Clinton also said, "The people who are most disappointed and beaten down have not known colossal failures. I've known colossal failures … " He smiled, and the audience chuckled with him.

We see from this comment that it's important to admit an event or tendency that has inspired you to learn to modify your behavior.

It is helpful to avoid trying to seem to be all things to all people. Focus on being the right person for the right job. For example, I have a extremely detail-conscious person provide editing for my books. I have artistic people work on the illustrations of my graphic novels including *Jack AngelSword.* And I have an intuitive person, who has not read all the books I've read, who listens to a first draft of my writing. She can point out details that may need expansion.

Everyone has weaknesses. Not all weaknesses can be eliminated. The effective person makes good choices and finds ways to compensate for weaknesses.

Talent is cheaper than table salt. What separates the talented individual from the successful one is a lot of hard work.
– Stephen King

What is the hard work? Rehearsal! Rehearse before the job interview.

Prepare anecdotes of actions you've taken in previous jobs, to highlight what a great team player you are. Avoid the self- aggrandizing, self-absorbed comments that smart but arrogant people say during job interviews. Mention a few appropriate details about how your team members did well and how you supported their efforts and initiatives. In this way, you can give the impression that you are a personable and competent team player.

Prepare for tough questions. My clients learn to gain "think-space," so that they can think before they answer. Here are some phrases you can use to give yourself some think-space:

1. "When you ask that question, it reminds me of ... "

2. "I can see you are concerned about that, and I'll need to pause (think) for a moment. I want to make sure that I give you a valuable answer ... "

3. "I haven't looked at it this way before. I'm interested in that, too. I'll need to look into it over the next one or two days."

Principle: Prepare for the tough questions and rehearse.

Power Question: What are the questions that make you squirm? Write these questions down and note three possible answers to each one. Rehearse with friends to see what responses feel real and appropriate to you.

Just before you go into an interview, review the company's annual report. Take a look at the firm's Web site. Review the company's press releases. Review your notes from people in the organization whom you've interviewed on your own. With all the details fresh in your mind, you will come across as a confident person who has the firm's interests at heart.

Use a mnemonic device to help you remember crucial details. For example, you can use the letters of N.E.W. to remember key words, such as New product; Early adopters; and Why I want to work here. You can also hold a 3-by-5 card of key notes in your hand.

Some of my clients hesitate to use the 3-by-5 card during an interview. To handle this situation, I encourage them to have a phrase like this ready: "I just have a couple of notes here, because there are a few details that I know can be helpful during our discussion." In this way, they are ready for the interviewer's quizzical look at their 3-by-5 card.

Principle: Review just before the interview.

Power Questions: What areas of your preparation feel fuzzy at the moment? How can you "get solid" about those details? Can you create a mnemonic device?

Engage Connection

How important is a resume? Often, it is simply a tool to get the interview. During the interview, you must use excellent first impression skills. When I speak on the topic "First Impressions Are Everything: Break the Two-Second Barrier and Influence People," I emphasize the Power-Three of Influence.

The Power-Three of Influence:

1. Show how much you care.

2. Show that you and your interviewer have common concerns, traits and feelings.

3. Demonstrate that you're a trusted advisor.

A journalist asked, "Trusted advisor?"

I replied, "Yes. Every good co-worker is called upon to voice a hypothesis or learned opinion as the team solves problems."

To influence the interviewer to give you a job, you want to do things that help create the Power-Three of Influence. You are seeking a "me, too" moment. For example, if two people find that they are both parents, they might make a connection, a moment of understanding. But avoid "me, too—one up." If the interviewer says that she has one son, avoid mentioning that you have three sons.

To help you prepare in advance for the interview, draw up a list of possible ways to connect with a new person. To construct this list, you need to reflect about various facets of your life and your own preferences. Also, see if you can get some information about the interviewer (through Google, for example) before your meeting.

Principle: Connection is crucial.

Power Questions: How can you feel comfortable about connecting? Have you identified 20 possible ways that you can connect with a new person?

Save Money for Last

When George Takei (Sulu of *Star Trek*) first met Gene Roddenberry (the creator of *Star Trek*) in an informal meeting, Gene was late.

"I hope it wasn't too long," Gene said.

"Oh no, not at all," George replied politely.

"How do you pronounce that last name of yours?" Gene asked, just after he'd mispronounced the name as "Tah-K-eye."

George replied that it rhymes with okay.

"Oh, okay. Takei as in okay. Takei is okay." Gene laughed.

George flowed in the moment and mentioned that the other way Gene pronounced his name was a "legitimate Japanese word."

"Really? What does it mean?" Gene asked. "Well, it translates into English as 'expensive.'"

"Oh, my God! I'd better make sure I call you Takei. Takei is definitely okay," Gene laughed.

In this conversation, George demonstrated a lighthearted way to create a connection and help the other person feel comfortable.*

(* NOTE: As a sidenote, years ago, George Takei taught me something about filmmaking. I showed him some feature film storyboards, and he saw a shot in which a character's tear flowed down and splashed in his teacup. George said gently, "Uh, Tom, isn't that a bit melodramatic?" Yes, George, I never filmed it. Thanks.)

Talking about money often makes people uncomfortable. In a job interview, it is best to discuss salary after you have proved your value to the company.

If the interviewer starts the meeting with, "What are your salary requirements?" you need to have some effective possible responses ready. You could reply, "Oh, you're offering me the position?"

At that point, the interviewer usually backs off and says, "Not yet. Let's continue with the interview."

Another response to the early "salary requirements" question is, "My salary requirements are in line with the market rates connected to my experience and skills. How about we continue talking about how I fit in with this team and how I can be of service?"

The interviewer is looking for ways to screen you out. You need to first prove your value to the firm. Researchers report that firms will often create a new or modified position when they know the special skills of a particular candidate. The point is, avoid discussing salary until you know that the firm wants you.

The secret to making $1,000 a minute in a job interview

A number of authors have discussed this powerful method to help you gain a higher salary. Practice this pattern with a friend before you have a job interview in which salary will be discussed.

The $1,000-a-minute pattern

Interviewer: "We're prepared to offer you $40,000." Janet: "Hmmm. $40,000."

(Then Janet is silent. She waits—even if she's just thinking of her phone number backwards. Her facial expression gives the impression that she is thinking about the offer.)

Interviewer: "Um … uh … Perhaps we could go to $45,000."

Janet: "$45,000 … "

(Janet is silent again. She waits.)

Interviewer: "Okay, okay. $50,000 is the best we can do. It really is our last offer."

(Janet notices all the clues in the situation and decides that this truly is the last offer.)

Janet: "Great! I'm really looking forward to working here."

Janet has just made $10,000 in three minutes.

The important keys to the $1,000-a-minute pattern:

1. *Repeat the figure* so the interviewer knows you heard it.

2. *Be silent.* Let the silence push the interviewer to the next step.

3. *In many first-impression situations, you can show your good character by listening.* During a salary negotiation, the prospective employee creates the first impression that the employer receives. She shows confidence, poise and knowledge of her own value (and the effort she'll devote to the job). The interviewer thinks, "She must be good. Her confidence shows it. She held out for nearly the top of our salary range."

Let's remember, the interviewer is looking for a bargain—a valuable worker for a reasonable salary. This pattern of silent waiting is gentle enough so that you do not appear unreasonable in your salary demands. Rehearse the pattern.

Important warning: Sometimes it is best to avoid negotiating. No method is appropriate for all situations. Some situations call for us to *avoid* negotiating. If you are going into a new field, you might be better off to take a modest salary for the chance to get started in the industry. There are times when we have a deep intuitive feeling ("I had this gut feeling") that we should be working at a particular company. It might be important for you to just get in the door and take a modest position with a modest salary. Numerous case studies show how successful people started in the mailroom or as an assistant, and then made sure that they were in the right place at the right time.

Remember to prepare and rehearse for your job interview.

Principle: Save the money discussion for last, after you've proved what a terrific asset you would be to the team.

Power Questions: Are you willing to risk losing the position just to gain some more money? Are you at the point in your career at which you're aiming to "trade up"? Be brutally honest with yourself. Do you have the skills and finesse to be highly desirable to a new employer? If not, what can you do this week to improve your skills and gain relevant experience?

Part VII
Negotiate Your Way to Success

Let's remember to be kind to ourselves, as we would be kind to a friend. Do you remember a time when you asked a friend, "What do you want?" When your friend replied, "tea," or anything else, you were happy to help. So pull out your personal journal and ask yourself, "What do you want?" Then go one step deeper. Ask yourself, "What do you want to feel?"

Your Least Acceptable Result (LAR) is the minimal deal that you will accept. As long as you do better than your LAR, you know you're successful. For example, a speaker whose regular fee is $9,000 may agree to accept $6,000 when she wants to enter a new market. If her LAR was $4,000, then she's still done well.

When you flinch at the first offer, you are likely to get a better result for yourself, and the other person will feel better in the long run. How is this possible?

Here is an example: Trudy considers purchasing a used car that is advertised at $3,000. She offers $1,000. The car owner immediately accepts. Does Trudy feel good?

No. She thinks, (a) "what's wrong with the car?" and (b) "I could have done better." It would have been better for the car owner to flinch at the first offer and express discomfort.

Negotiation, sales, and many forms of business relations depend on rapport. *The Merriam-Webster's Medical Dictionary* defines "rapport" as (1) relation characterized by harmony, conformity, accord, or affinity; (2) confidence of a subject in the operator (as in hypnotism, psychotherapy, or mental testing) with willingness to cooperate.

When I speak on details related to negotiating and sales, I share the A.C.T.I.O.N. process:

A – Approach them in ways they prefer
C – Communicate vividly
T – Touch them five times
I— Invite action
O – Open to personal value
N – Note value and gratitude

Approach Them in Ways They Prefer

How do you know how a person prefers to be approached? Now, that is a powerful question.

First, let's notice that every person has a preferred way to be approached. We take in new information through different modalities: audio, visual, and kinesthetic (touch).

Some people prefer to—
1. Hear a phone call
2. See someone face to face
3. Read an e-mail message
4. Read a postcard

How do you find out how a person prefers a first contact? You observe and listen. At a networking event, you can hear people's preferences in their offhand comments:

• "I get about 90 e-mail messages a day. It takes so much time to go through them … "

• "I hate those awful faxes that are just advertisements. What a waste of paper!"

We have just learned that approaching these individuals through e-mail or a fax might cause hard feelings. So we can seek another way to create connection.

We need to focus on two crucial details when approaching someone:
1. Be respectful, and
2. Approach the person with something that can help him or her.

Be respectful

At a number of my speeches, audience members can enter a drawing for one of my products. Even if they do not win the product, they can choose to receive an e-newsletter, Success Secrets, and an e-book. Audience members fill out a rating sheet that respectfully offers them the options to choose to receive the e-newsletter and e-book. The whole interaction is about my giving them continued value. This is respectful.

Approach the person with something that can help him or her.

If you have any hesitation in approaching someone, get

clear on the benefit you are offering. Let this be your central question: "How can I help this person (so the by-product is that she will take the action I prefer)?" What value do you offer? You know that you will work hard, be on time, and avoid complaining. You will give great value for the opportunity to perform. This reminds me of an idea that relates to manifesting wealth: "I am here only to be truly helpful."

Give the person "permission"

We often see people hesitate even when they truly want something. We can help the person by providing the atmosphere of permission. The way we subtly help things flow along is to use such language as, "When you are using this (product) …" With such a statement, you are basically assuming that the sale has been made. You are demonstrating your confidence that the person will close the deal with you.

Finally, there are times when we do not know what the best approach to someone will be. Then we look for a good approach, one that involves both being respectful and offering something helpful.

Principle:

People have a preferred way to receive information: visual, auditory, or kinesthetic (touch).

Power Questions:

How can you discover the person's preferred way of taking in information? Can you participate in a group discussion so you can hear her comments? Can you talk with her assistant? Can you read a book or interview she's done? (Use Google.com to find any articles posted on the Internet.)

Communicate Vividly

If a [person] would move the world, he must first move himself.
– Socrates

In order to communicate powerfully with people, you need to communicate clearly with yourself.

Ask yourself:

- What do I really want?
- How important is this to me?
- What do I need to learn here?

Armed with the answers to these questions, you are ready to communicate vividly. Use the following general principles:

Use word pictures

Use word pictures, a personal story, and an appeal to the emotions. Remember that people tend to buy on emotion and then justify their decision on fact. Word pictures create an image. For example, a friend can say, "When I was waiting for you, I felt like a puppy cast adrift in a tiny raft in the middle of the huge ocean."

Here's an example of how a personal story invited people to give to a foundation. A friend sent me and many others an e-mail message about how a certain foundation had sent his loved one a monthly stipend to help with her rent and living expenses when she was incapacitated by a disease. This story was effective because we all knew the person and appreciated how the foundation had helped during her time of need.

Use the salted oats process

Another way to communicate vividly is based on the salted oats process. Author Stephen Scott, in his book *Simple Steps to Impossible Dreams,* tells the story of how to lead a horse to water and ensure that he drinks. You put salt into his oats, to make him thirsty.

In conversation, one sets the stage so that the listener eagerly awaits certain details. Here's an example:

Susan: "This reminds me of something Lynda Obst (producer of *Sleepless in Seattle*) said about going into meetings with film finance people. She had a special strategy that she learned from Peter Guber. Would you like to hear about it?"

Deanna: "Yes. This sounds interesting."

Use the Principles of Influence

In his book *Influence*, researcher/author Robert Cialdini noted the principles of influence, including:

1. Reciprocity
2. Commitment and consistency
3. Social proof
4. Perception of scarcity
5. Liking
6. Authority

Let's look at these in more detail...

Strategy 1: Create reciprocity

Reciprocity occurs when one person gives something and the other person feels compelled to return the favor. Bestselling author Roger Dawson tells the story of asking someone at an airport for change so he could make a 25 cent phone call. The man gave Roger a quarter, and Roger gave him one dollar and then had to run for his plane. The man and his family followed Roger across the airport, trying to give him his change. Their feelings of fairness were pronounced.

The principle of reciprocity is the basis of my encouraging you throughout this book to help someone first. You will stand out as a helpful and genuinely kind human being. In my book, *Relax Your Way Networking,* I share what I call **The 3 Magic Words of Networking: Help Them First.**

Strategy 2: Use the commitment & consistency principle

When people commit to something small, they are likely to follow through because they want to feel and appear to be consistent in their actions. This is like the flow of the martial art aikido. The aikido master gently leads the opponent in the direction in which the opponent is already going.

Notice these options:

Question: "Susan, how can we stay in contact?"

Person's Reply: "I'm sorry—I'm out of cards."

Answer: "Oh, I'll make one for you." (You pull out one of your business cards and write the person's contact information on the back. I crease the edge to *avoid* accidentally giving away the card with the person's contact information.)

Question: "Do you have e-mail at yahoo.com or gmail.com?"

All these questions flow forward to the goal of getting an e-mail address. This idea is to invite someone to do something small; the anonymous e-mail of Yahoo.com or gmail.com is a small commitment. Most of the time, the person will give a personal e-mail address. He or she was already flowing in that direction.

Strategy 3: Demonstrate social proof

When bestselling author Tony Robbins bought a large mansion ("a castle"), he created social proof that his methods yield tremendous rewards. When giving a seminar in North Hollywood, California, I encouraged who are actors to place photos of their television and film appearances on their Web sites. In the minds of casting decision-makers, such photos create the impression, "She must be good. All these other professionals have cast her. She's always working."

Strategy 4: Enhance the perception of scarcity

People often want what they can't have. In sales, it's called the take-away close. For example, a real estate person selling a house might say, "Oh no! I just saw something in my notes. I may not be able to offer this house to you. I have a note here that says the owner was talking with another buyer. I'm sorry." Suddenly, the buyer finds that she wants the house more. She has the perception of scarcity. (By the way, if you are concerned that this method may be manipulative, please see my book, *Darkest Secrets of Persuasion and Seduction Masters: How to Protect Yourself and Turn the Power to Good.*)

Create an impression that you're not waiting by the phone. People want to work with those professionals who are highly sought after by others.

Strategy 5: Set the stage for you to be liked

People will do a lot for a friend. In directing a feature film, I expanded the part of the little girl who portrayed the daughter of the main character because I liked her and her parents. They were a joy to work with. I had no hesitation in rewriting the script to expand her part.

On the other hand, I have worked with people who were disruptive. I arranged the schedules so that they were off my movie set quickly.

Being likeable is a big component in getting a job, a movie role and other opportunities. (You can call this the liking factor.) How can you encourage someone new to like you?

Use the L.I.K.E.–M.E.–N.O.W. process:

L – Listen
I – Interview
K – Kindle similarity
E – Express gratitude
M – Monitor time
E – Engage the person's concerns
N – Note ideal clients
O – Open to humor
W – Watch and help

Listen - Listen first. Ask a gentle question such as, "So, how do you know our host, Matt?"

Interview - You can easily start a conversation and put the person at ease. I often ask, "What are your hobbies?" This is a valuable question because people frequently enjoy their hobbies more than their current jobs. Or you can ask, "What are you looking forward to?"

Kindle similarity - A conversation warms up when people have a "Me, too!" moment. You often you hear this kind of comment: "Oh, you like skiing, too? What's your favorite resort?"

Express gratitude - You can say, "Thanks for your time," or "Thank you for your efforts on this one." In an e-mail, it often helps to begin with "Thank you for ... "

Monitor time - Respect the person's time. Say things like, "This will be quick. I know you're busy."

Engage the person's concerns - Ask gentle questions to find out what is causing pain or inconvenience for the person. Then you can show how you hold similar concerns. This creates connection.

Note ideal clients - You can ask, "Who's your ideal client?" or "Are you looking for specific types of people? Perhaps I can help send some folks your way."

Open to humor - Humor is something to be careful about. In fact, in my book *10 Seconds to Wealth,* I cover 30 Secrets of Humor. I emphasize that it is helpful to observe what the person finds funny and flow with it if possible. One author states that the people he loves are the ones he laughs with.

Watch and help - You can ask, "How can I support what you're doing?" This is a better question than "How can I help you?" because many of us recoil when hearing a salesperson ask that question in a store.

Strategy 6: Inspire compliance with authority

A number of people are conditioned to comply with requests by an authority figure. For example, years ago at a certain training weekend, a seminar leader required that people not leave the room to use the restroom. Then the seminar leader said, "So, we have agreed on our rules." Because the leader was the authority figure, many people automatically nodded their heads. But one man stood up and said, "No. Those are your rules. I have not agreed." With that, he left the auditorium. The other people remained.

Researchers note that many people still react through the conditioning they have received since childhood to comply with an authority figure's demands. Let's look at two points. First, we can make sure to pay attention so that we do not respond to unreasonable demands solely because of our conditioning. Second, if we are in a position of authority, we can do things to strengthen that position of influence.

A number of authors noted that President Jimmy Carter did certain things that seemed to undermine the authority of the Presidency during his term in office. He was seen carrying his own baggage into the White House. On the other hand, President Ronald Reagan did many things to strengthen the image of the presidency. He always wore his suit jacket, unlike previous presidents, who had been more casual in the Oval Office.

Principle: To influence someone, focus on helping her in some way.

Power Question: What gentle questions do you feel comfortable asking? How can you gently discover ways that you can help the person?

Touch Them Five Times

Be like water making its way through cracks … You put water into a bottle and it becomes the bottle. You put it in a teapot; it becomes the teapot. Now, water can flow or it can crash. Be water, my friend. – Bruce Lee

Water can touch an object in many places. Similarly, researchers have noted that in order to close a transaction, it's necessary to ask an average of five to nine times.

Have at least five ways to ask for the sale:

1. So, you're ready to go forward with this?
2. This will work for you, right?
3. Would you okay this? (instead of: Sign here)
4. How about we take care of the paperwork now?
5. You'd like delivery when?

Part of the five touches can be just staying in touch. That is, you demonstrate that you are a nice, helpful person. People tend to do business with people they like.

Principle: Ask for the sale five times, gently.

Power Question: What are five different ways to ask for the sale (or agreement) that are comfortable for you?

Invite Action

How can you avoid a person's resistance? Gently invite her to act. As you hand her a pen to sign the agreement, say,

"Would you okay this?" Avoid the phrase "please sign this." To okay something is gentle. On the other hand, to "sign this" is scary.

The answer is always 'no' if you don't ask.

– Patricia Fripp and Tony Robbins, noted by both

Again, the strategy is to pre-plan five methods or ways to ask to close the sale.

"If you don't ask, you don't get." – Mahatma Gandhi

Some novice salespersons hesitate to ask because they are afraid of being intrusive. If you are a salesperson in a store, the people there have already placed themselves where they can buy some- thing, so you are being helpful. In fact, years ago when I was trained in retail sales, I learned to say, **"So, what brings you into the store today?"** This was better than the annoying "May I help you?"

You can invite action gently by asking, "How would this product improve your daily life?" Then follow up with a minor detail such as, "Would you like it in blue?" This is a subtle way to invite action.

Principle: If you don't ask, you don't get.

Power Question: Which friend or family member can help you rehearse ways to smoothly and comfortably invite the buyer to take action?

Open to Personal Value

Imagine if I could give you a method that would ensure that you could get what you really want. Interested?

I have just demonstrated the power of zeroing in on what someone wants on a personal level. People buy on emotion. ("What's in it for me?") Then they justify their purchase based on facts.

When you help someone to open his or her perspective to a personal gain with your product, you can be doing that person a favor.

All the money in the world is spent on feeling good. - Ry Cooder

Researchers note that people make decisions for reasons related to personal gain. Superstar salespeople do not ask solely how the buyer's company will profit. These superstars help the prospective buyer imagine the personal benefit of a "yes" answer. To do this, ask a question like, "If the product does just what you need it to do, how do you benefit personally?"

If the buyer responds, "My boss will like the fact that I handled the problem," you have the fuel to move toward the next step. The personal gain may be a happy boss who retains the employee during layoffs, or who will be inclined to offer the employee a raise or promotion.

If you are talking with a sole proprietor, you can say, "When you use (the product), you'll save $3,000 in the first two weeks." Remember to discover what is most important to the prospective customer on a personal level.

Principle: To get the person to say yes, create an experience of how he or she will personally benefit.

Power Questions: How can you ask gentle questions so that you identify how the person will personally benefit from saying yes? How can you help the person experience (imagine) a personal benefit?

Note Value and Gratitude

Remind the person of the value and benefits she will enjoy now that she has agreed to your proposal. This helps the sale or negotiated agreement stay solid. Remember, each sale or negotiated agreement is ideally part of a good long-term business relationship.

The second point is to effectively thank the person for working with you. People appreciate a heartfelt "thank you." The crucial thing to remember is that each individual has a preferred way to receive appreciation and gratitude.

Along this line, while researching how people build healthy relationships, I discovered Dr. Gary Chapman's book, *The Five Love Languages*. In this book, Gary Chapman points out that each person has a personal "love language." If you speak the person's language, he or she will truly experience your gratitude.

The five love languages:
1. Words of affirmation
2. Gifts
3. Quality time
4. Acts of service
5. Physical touch

Our goal is to appropriately and effectively express gratitude and create positive feelings.

You want to express your gratitude in a way the person can readily accept and feel. Here are examples related to the love languages:

Words of affirmation - "Joe, thanks for all your efforts. You were really effective in finding solutions to help our two teams work together. Thank you."

Gifts - A small, appropriate gift that relates to the person's hobby can be helpful. It's great when we honor people this way.

Quality time - When meeting with a new customer, turn off your cell phone. When someone acts as though taking a cell phone call is more important than talking to us, it hurts. Don't let this happen with your new customer.

Acts of service - Often, a customer will appreciate receiving an article that relates to the hobby of her son or daughter. In this way, you can enrich your business relationship with the customer. The idea of service is that you extend an extra effort for the other person's well-being.

Physical touch - Each person needs to be careful about this detail of touching. If the new customer has extended his or her hand for a good handshake, then you can shake hands.

Remember, the idea is to effectively express gratitude and create good, friendly feelings.

Principle: Develop business relationships. Help the person feel good by showing the value gained through your presence and by expressing your gratitude.

Power Questions: How can you gently remind the person of the value he or she has gained? How can you express your gratitude?

Part VII
Be Heard and Be Trusted on the Telephone

What if you could change your life with one phone call? And what if you had the skills to make that phone call go extremely well?

One phone call changed the life of Michael Eisner, former CEO of the Walt Disney Company. Years ago, Frank Wells, who would become the president and COO of the Walt Disney Company, said to Michael, "It's over. Sid [Bass] isn't buying," referring to the largest shareholder in the Disney Company. Michael Eisner had been Frank Wells' choice for the job of CEO—the top leadership position in the company —but he and Frank both knew that without Sid's backing, Michael did not have a chance.

Michael wanted to take another shot at the job. He made a call to Sid, who was at his Fort Worth office. On the speakerphone, Michael said, "I think you're making a mistake, Sid. It's going to take a creative person to run this company. Look at the history of America's companies. They have always gotten into trouble when the creative people at the top are replaced by managers."

Sid hesitated. Then he realized that the Disney Company needed someone who would have the decisiveness and the freedom to choose those projects he thought best for the company. Sid later recalled, "Michael has to have the final word. That's when I first thought Michael was CEO material."

Michael became the top leader, Chairman and Chief Executive. It was a dream come true for him, because Walt Disney had been Michael's personal hero. What we learn from Michael's effort is that he persisted in the face of apparent defeat, and he effectively communicated his passion for the job.

Successful people are great communicators. All of us can make efforts to improve our communication skills.

The challenge with the telephone is that you have fewer tools—only your voice, with no facial expression or body language.

I shared the following ideas when I presented this topic: "Telephone Power: Sell More and Convert Irate Customers into Customers Referring Business."

We will use the P.H.O.N.E. process:

P – Practice smiling
H – Honor personality styles
O – Own your energy level
N – Note timing
E – Earn her trust

Practice Smiling

Researchers have demonstrated that people can hear a

smile on the phone. So, smile! And stand up; you will sound confident and energetic. Use a mirror. It will remind you to lighten up before you pick up the phone receiver.

One day, I called a company to register myself and my team member for a seminar. That's it. All I wanted to do was register two people. But before a minute went by, I found myself purchasing a book and asking if there were any other products I should know about.

As soon as the salesperson answered the phone, her tone of voice told me, "I'm happy to be talking with you. Your call is the most important one of my day. I'm here to help you take your business to the next level." She immediately put me at ease and gently guided me to purchase more; that is, she let me see how I could gain more benefits from the company's products. It was a good thing for me that she wasn't selling houses!

If you have zest and enthusiasm you attract zest and enthusiasm. Life does give back in kind. – Norman Vincent Peale

When you practice smiling, you practice placing yourself in a better state of being.

Principle: A smile can be heard on the phone.

Power Questions: How will you place a mirror near your phone? Will you use a Post-It Note with the word "smile," too?

Honor Personality Styles

If your caller talks quietly, talk quietly. Match her tone. A person who talks loudly may feel that someone who speaks softly is untrustworthy. People tend to trust people who talk in a similar fashion as they do.

By agreeing that whatever [the person is] experiencing is valid, you create rapport … It's this rapport that melts resistance. People don't like to feel alone. They want someone on their side. A friend

is easier to buy from than a salesperson or marketer. Be a friend.
  – *Joe Vitale*

Researchers have identified four personality styles. Over the years, I have seen that audience members find it easier to remember the styles when I give them animal labels:

- Lion
- Beaver
- Dog
- Peacock

Below are descriptions of these personality styles, which I revealed in my book *Darkest Secrets of Persuasion and Seduction Masters: How to Protect Yourself and Turn the Power to Good.*

Lion: A hard-charging leader, who may be considered abrupt or bossy.

Beaver: An analytical person, who likes tables, graphs and lots of details. This person wants to appear intelligent

and makes decisions slowly due to a great fear of making a mistake.

Dog: A supporter, who likes routine and cares about the feelings of others. This person may be slow to accept change.

Peacock: An extrovert, who loves to stand out in a crowd and gain approval. This person may be ineffective when it comes to follow-up.

The solution is to identify what your personality style is.

Then you can get your own preoccupations out of the way and speak in a way that will immediately make the other person feel comfortable. For example, if you are a hard-charging person and are talking with someone who has a Dog personality style, it helps to ask how he or she is first, before launching into the conversation.

The following will help you adapt to your listener's personality style, it lists what you should tone down in different circumstances.

Lion addressing Dog: Ask how the Dog is first. Tone down your fast-paced, intense talking style.

Dog addressing Lion: Go directly to the point and talk about the bottom line. Tone down any of your comments that may reveal "weakness" in the Lion's eyes.

Lion addressing Beaver: Let the Beaver give you some details, or identify which topics you would welcome details about. Tone down your need to talk quickly and move on.

Beaver addressing Lion: Identify three possible solutions and ask the Lion if she wants any particular details. Tone down your need to provide all the details.

Beaver addressing Peacock: Provide details that help the Peacock "look good." Tone down your disdain for "flashy people" or "hype."

This is a first look at how you can relate to a personality style that contrasts with your own style.

Apply the elements of personality styles so that you can match the person's tone, volume and pacing. Each personality style has a distinctive sound. Furthermore, many people feel that tone is related to attitude.

Here is a table of how tone, volume, and pacing (speed of speech) relate to personality styles.

Personality Styles:

Lion:
  (Tone) Intense
  (Volume) Loud
  (Pacing) Fast

Dog:
  (Tone) Soft
  (Volume) Soft
  (Pacing) Slower

Beaver:
  (Tone) Precise
  (Volume) Medium
  (Pacing) Slower
Peacock
  (Tone) Energetic * (Volume) Loud * (Pacing) Might Be
  Fast

Practicing with friends or a coach can help you make the transitions to different tones and pacing. The idea is to rehearse so that you can easily adapt to the sound of the new person. Then you can be heard and be trusted.

Principle: Match the person's tone, volume and pacing.

Power Questions: How will you arrange times and ways to rehearse matching a caller's tone, volume and pacing? Which friends can help you?

Own Your Energy Level

When do people change a habit? They change when they own a problem. Owning a problem means acknowledging that they have a problem and that they can do something to make things better.

Each individual needs to identify what brings his or her energy level up or down. If a customer brings your energy down, then do what works for you: take a walk to the water cooler, step outside and walk around the block, or close your eyes briefly and take a few deep breaths.

The ancestor of every action is thought. - Ralph Waldo Emerson

The idea is for us to have useful thoughts that come to our minds by reflex. Here are two helpful thoughts:

1. Next! (if you are selling something and the person shows absolutely no interest). This is a powerful word because it reminds us that there are other people to connect

with, and it is likely that they will be a better match for what we're offering.

2. Oh, you're the one in 100! I have 99 nice people to talk with next. This helps avoid letting one negative interaction slow you down.

If you notice that you're craving a candy bar, you can assess what helpful thought can relate to that. Perhaps you need a change of pace. You can energize yourself by walking to the water cooler and having water—and you'll avoid the after-candy-bar crash in energy.

Principle: Discover your own healthy ways to raise your tone and energy level.

Power Questions: What raises your tone and energy level? How can you make sure to put in breaks and short transition times during your workday?

Note Timing
Timing in life is everything. – Leonard Maltin

"Is this a good time to talk?" can be a crucial question to begin a phone call. When we call, we have no idea what state of being the person is in.

Throughout the phone conversation, note how the person sounds. Is she tired? Is she too busy to take this call? Is she distracted? If so, ask what would be a good time for you to call back.

It is the mark of an educated [person] to be able to evaluate a thought without accepting it. – Aristotle

Similarly, it is the mark of the educated person to note a personal feeling and be able to flow past it. That is, you can note the urgent feeling, "I must get a meeting with this person." Then you can reply to yourself, "Okay. I hear you (you acknowledge your feeling). And I'm more likely to get the meeting by respecting her and accommodating her feelings."

This internal dialogue can occur in seconds, and it can shift how you feel. This is crucial because how you feel affects how you sound (your tonality). So it is helpful to practice asking a prospective customer, "Is this a good time to talk?" before you call the person.

Principle: Find out whether the timing of your call is agreeable.

Power Question: Which ways of asking whether it's a good time to talk feel appropriate to you?

Earn Her Trust

I long to accomplish a great and noble task, but it is my chief duty to accomplish small tasks as if they were great and noble.
– Helen Keller

Do the correct small tasks and do them in a respectful manner, and you can earn someone's trust. You can follow this pattern even when you cold-call someone:

"Hello, Susan. Janet Smith said that it would be great for us to connect. My firm provides training to help salespeople double their sales. I'm Carol Wenzil, and I'm the president of Wenzil & Associates. Is this a good time to talk?"

Carol earned trust in these ways: (a) She began with a personal referral, (b) She expressed a benefit: doubling Susan's sales, and (c) She asked, "Is this a good time to talk?" (expressing respect for the person's time and comfort).

The friendly person is

1. Respectful
2. A good listener
3. Helpful

If you get an intuitive feeling that you would do well to call a particular customer or prospective customer, make the call as soon as possible. You may be calling at just the right time to be a friend. Perhaps a business transaction has gone south for her, and your solution is just what she needs.

A real friend is one who walks in when the rest of the world walks out. – Walter Winchell

Remember, earn your listener's trust.

Principle: Without trust, nothing can move forward.

Power Question: How can you immediately establish that you are caring and trustworthy?

Part VIII
How to Use Your Brand as Your Shortcut to Trust

Do you ever buy the brand-name product? Why? Perhaps you feel that you can trust the product.

When you want to expand your firm's prosperity, you will be interested in the process of making a brand name. Researchers point out that there are certain actions that create a well-received brand.

In Walt Disney World, a little girl was eating an ice cream cone while standing in line for an attraction. Just before she stepped aboard the ride, one of the attendants said, "I'm sorry. You can't bring the ice cream on the ride." The little girl cried. Her parents looked on with concern. Then the attendant said, "I can hold the ice cream cone for you until you come back from the ride." The little girl stopped crying and said, "Okay." After the ride, the girl retrieved the ice cream cone from the attendant.

The important detail here is that the parents knew the original ice cream cone had melted in the hot Florida sun. They realized that while they were enjoying the ride, the attendant had run over to the ice cream stand for another cone. This story creates powerful positive feelings toward Walt Disney World and the Disney organization. What a vivid example of a trustworthy brand!

The vital detail I want to share here is STORY. That is, identify the stories that convey what your brand delivers as *benefits* to your customer.

Stories sell! Facts just tell. Help your delighted clients give you powerful mini-stories as testimonials, such as, "Joe's product helped me save $10,000 last month." Include client testimonials and partial client lists in all your marketing materials.

People go with their first impressions, so ensure that the first impression is favorable. Director James Cameron faced a big decision: who would he choose as the male lead for his blockbuster $200 million feature film *Titanic?* At first, Leonardo DiCaprio refused to audition for James. That could have been a real mistake, destroying Leo's opportunity to play Jack Dawson, the lead role in the film. But Leo had a second chance; he finally agreed to audition. James said, "Leo read the scene once, and then he got up and started goofing around ... but for one split second, a shaft of light came down from the heavens and lit up the forest." Even big mistakes can be overcome when you are known to perform at a high level prompting someone like James Cameron to offer a second chance.

Leo had other things going for him. For example, when Jim arrived late for their first, informal meeting at Jim's Lightstorm offices, he discovered that almost every female Lightstorm team member was in the conference room with Leo. Jim said, "Leo must be used to this, because he charmed everyone in the room." One week later, right after Kate Winslet (who played Rose) auditioned with Leo, she pulled

Cameron aside and told him, "Even if you don't hire me, you have to hire Leo."

James Cameron found Leo "incredibly mercurial," able to run ten different emotions through a scene. The 20th Century Fox executives were not sold on Leo to star in the film, even though they were seeing dailies of *Romeo + Juliet*. But James Cameron said, "I always trust my first impression. It sounds corny, but that's what the audience does."

Principle: Inspire powerful feelings in the buyer. This will help the person buy easily.

Power Questions: What are the powerful positive feelings associated with your product? What are the buyer's negative feelings that your product can eliminate?

Branding gives you the opportunity to become brand-new … Those things you're passionate about give you the best possible chance for success … What words come to mind when people say your name? – Robin Fisher Roffer

Form your brand strategically and communicate the benefits you offer.

Part IX
Great Communicators Make Good Luck

How do great communicators create good luck?

Great Communicators put people at ease, create connection, and then are offered more opportunities.

Think of lucky people you know and have heard about in the news or from other sources. You'll notice that lucky people are offered more opportunities than others are.

Anyone who is successful in any business who doesn't use the word 'luck' is a liar. Luck played a part in it. – Paul Newman to Larry King

Happiness often sneaks in through a door you didn't know you left open. – John Barrymore

By creating an atmosphere of good will, the great communicator leaves many doors open. People like to work with great communicators. They call them to offer projects. They give referrals.

The more valuable you become to more people, the more opportunities will open for you.

We will use the M.A.K.E.–L.U.C.K. process:

M – Make yourself prepared

A – Align your persuasion skills

K – Keep searching

E – Excel on another horse

L – Look to help

U – Use everything for networking

C – Course-correct constantly

K – Keep going for what you really want

Open the door to enjoyable opportunities!

Make Yourself Prepared

Spectacular achievement is always preceded by unspectacular preparation. – Robert H. Schuller

Would you like to know how Bill Gates took a few thousand dollars and translated them into a multi-billion dollar business? He used the power of information.

At a pivotal moment in PC history, Bill Gates knew three vital details:

1. IBM was looking for an operating system for its original computer.

2. Seattle Computer had created an operating system that it called Q-DOS.

3. Seattle Computer did not know of IBM's need and IBM

did not know of Seattle Computer.

Bill took action. He borrowed $50,000 from his father, bought Q-DOS, renamed it MS-DOS, and licensed it to IBM. These actions started the ball rolling toward a gain of billions of dollars.

Bill Gates has repeatedly demonstrated his attention to detail and preparation. This reminds us to prepare ourselves.

Similarly, Oprah Winfrey prepared herself to make the most of opportunities as they arrived. At age 19, Oprah became the first woman and first African-American to join Nashville's WTVF-TV as an anchor. Three years in that position became a springboard to a larger market, WJZ-TV in Baltimore. Then Oprah received a big disappointment: the 6 o'clock news producers decided that she reported news with too much emotion. The producers demoted her to the morning show, *People Are Talking.*

Some people might have labeled her dismissal from the evening news as a failure. Then something extraordinary happened. Oprah later said, "The minute the first show [*People Are Talking*] was over, I thought, 'Thank God, I've found what I was meant to do.' It's like breathing to me."

Oprah had found her niche. Within five years and after a personal crisis in Baltimore, Oprah had *The Oprah Winfrey Show* and was grossing $30 million. She was 30 years old with millions of fans.

Think like a queen. A queen is not afraid to fail. Failure is another steppingstone to greatness ... I do not believe in failure. It is not failure if you enjoyed the process. – Oprah Winfrey

Yes, Oprah found her niche. But she was always active. On the way to her niche, she kept looking for a way to contribute.

I think education is power. I think that being able to communicate with people is power. One of my main goals on the planet is to encourage people to empower themselves.
– Oprah Winfrey

Everything counts. The events of our life often add up to surprising benefits. Anna began playing the piano at age six. She went on to play the church organ.

Her parents had instilled in her a strong practical streak, so she graduated from college and went into computer programming. Yet music remained a powerful part of her life.

Anna also loved movies. She went to the movie theater at least once a week. One year, she teamed up with Maxine, a documentary filmmaker. Anna took the right risk and invested her money in computer equipment and synthesizers, which simulate the sounds of an entire orchestra. With this equipment, Anna created the music soundtrack for Maxine's documentary film. Now Anna is a motion picture soundtrack composer.

I've come to believe that each of us has a personal calling that's as unique as a fingerprint—and that the best way to succeed is to discover what you love and then find a way to offer it to others in the form of service, working hard, and also allowing the energy of the universe to lead you. – Oprah Winfrey

If you don't know exactly what you truly want to do, be comforted. It took around 35 years for Anna to discover her destiny. Anna went from the piano to computers, and then to composing with computers.

Everything you've done and everything you've learned contributes to your destiny. – Tom Marcoux

Do what you want to do on a small scale now. Practice your craft. Let's say an editor at a top publishing company calls me tomorrow and asks, "Can you write a 226-page book in three months?" I can reply "Yes!" because I've prepared for opportunities. I've practiced the art of writing for years. I also have experience in pushing myself to write on demand, which is a crucial skill. Having written 35 books, I can adapt my information to fit a new situation.

Many people say, "I could write a book." That may be true, but if they don't take action, they will never know. Training overcomes fear.

Continually prepare for the home run. – Tom Marcoux

A vital part of preparation is identifying what you truly want. Here are Marc Allen's comments on his startling discoveries about creating a life you truly love:

******Guest Article Below******

More Beyond Abundance to a Life of True Fulfillment by Marc Allen

The first step to discovering the secret of manifestation is to write your ideal scene on paper, your dream life five years in the future. Begin with the end in mind, and keep it in mind. The day I turned thirty, I sat down and took a sheet of paper and wrote Ideal Scene at the top. I imagined everything had gone as well as I could possibly imagine and somehow, over the next five years, I was able to create the ideal life for me. What would it look like? What would I do and have, and who would I be?

I was surprised, even shocked in a strange way, at what came spilling out on paper. I imagined I had a publishing company, successfully publishing books and music, including my own books and music. Before I sat down and wrote out my ideal scene, I had absolutely no interest in business. I had never taken a business course. I had never written a book or recorded my music. The words that spilled out when I wrote my ideal scene surprised me as much as they were to surprise just about everyone else I knew.

I imagined I wrote successful books and recorded beautiful music as well. I imagined I had a lovely white house on a hill in northern California, one of my favorite places on earth. I imagined I had a wonderfully loving relationship. I dared to imagine my ideal, so I imagined I had plenty of time for it all: creativity, a successful business, friends and family, and plenty of time alone for myself as well … That was my ideal: success with ease, and success without compromising the other things that were important to me in life …

The second step to discovering the secret of manifestation is to write your goals as affirmations, beginning with "In an easy and relaxed manner, in a healthy and positive way … " Years later, looking back, I realized how powerful those words were—so powerful, in fact, that by repeating them daily, I overcame many of my doubts and fears …

The next step to discovering the secret of manifestation is to write a one page plan for every major goal …

The final step to discovering the secret of manifestation is to take action …

We know the secret, deep in our hearts. We've always known the secret. To love one another and all of creation, is the greatest secret of all. Love overcomes fear, and transforms our lives and our world.

Marc Allen, publisher, author of *The Greatest Secret of All: Moving Beyond Abundance to a Life of True Fulfillment*, and cofounder of New World Library.
www.MarcAllen.com

Talking with and listening to Marc Allen has transformed my life. I have brought happy moments into my life by holding the idea of " … success with ease … in an easy and relaxed manner, in a healthy and positive way … " I invite you to re-read Marc's comments and implement his suggestions. Your possibilities will expand.

Principle: Devote time and effort daily to preparing for upcoming opportunities.

Power Question: What might be a terrific opportunity that you need to prepare for now—before such an opportunity is offered?

Align Your Persuasion Skills

What if you could get what you want without needing to persuade anyone? You'd be living in Fantasyland.

Our modern life is noisy and filled with distractions. Researchers estimate that we are bombarded with thousands advertising messages a day. For anyone to cooperate with you, they need to hear you. To make good luck, we need to be heard and to persuade.

The most important persuasion tool you have in your entire arsenal is integrity. – Zig Ziglar

"I don't like selling!" many people proclaim, almost like a badge of honor. To align yourself with persuasion skills is to let go of your limiting beliefs and empower yourself. For many people, the dislike of selling is really about three things:

• The dislike of rejection
• The dislike of manipulating someone
• The dislike of being seen as a manipulator

There is a solution. You can view positive selling as coaching someone. Let's remember what a coach does: she encourages you to do something for your benefit. A coach persuades you that it is worth your effort to make a change, take a risk, or stretch yourself. In a sense, Mahatma Gandhi coached or persuaded the British Empire to release its hold on the people of India. He succeeded.

Our focus here is on persuading with integrity. Integrity implies wholeness. In order to persuade with integrity, your heart and good will must be included.

To make your luck, you need to be able to help other people experience the value of participating in what you're offering. So let's replace "I don't like selling" with "I like coaching people to action."

The best salesperson is a trusted advisor. Let's say that Sam wants to make his luck by making a small, independent feature film. He persuades actors to work with him by emphasizing the benefits they will enjoy: an excellent demo reel and valuable work experience. He tells them that when established producers see the finished film, the actors will be more likely to gain other roles. For example, it was after Robert De Niro saw the actor Joe Pesci in a small feature film that Pesci gained the part of De Niro's brother in the film *Raging Bull.*

The key to successful persuasion is this:

Only speak of details that you know will definitely benefit and appeal to the person you're persuading.

Persuasion is most important when you're persuading yourself. When you want good luck, more money and feelings of fulfillment, who is the most important person you need to persuade? You!

Many of us truly feel that there are elements in life more important than money. Love, health and friendship come to mind. Furthermore, it is possible to earn money with integrity. You can put your heart into activities that earn money and align with your talents and interests.

Sometimes, it takes a couple of years of free-lance or part-time work to make the transition into doing what you love as your livelihood. From a place of integrity, one can choose to find methods of creating significant benefits for other people. As a by-product, these methods can bring financial abundance.

Some years ago, I was feeling overwhelmed. As I mentioned earlier, I told my sweetheart, "I'm like a racehorse." She replied, "Run in better races." Her comment got me thinking about how I could multiply the benefits I have to offer. This led me to realize,

You've got to be in the game where a big payday is possible.
– Tom Marcoux

If you want to make a leap forward and bring financial abundance into your life, you need to persuade yourself that you can gain new skills. For example, Jolene, a dishwasher, has a physical limit on how many dishes she can wash per hour. However, if she learns entrepreneurial skills and opens one restaurant, then another, she can greatly expand the financial abundance that flows into her life.

The process of persuading yourself often requires that you look for breakthrough ideas. Bestselling author and highly-paid speaker David Bach offers:

The market doesn't pay you what you're worth—it pays you what it has to ... and what you're willing to accept! – David Bach

The bottom-line real reason I am able to charge 10 times more today for virtually the exact same speech I gave five years ago is simply I decided to charge more ... I kept stretching my comfort level and raising my fee ... – David Bach

To make good luck happen, learn to persuade positively. Persuade yourself that what you offer is of tremendous value to your customer. Become a coach-to-action for yourself.

Principle: Convert the idea of "selling" into "coaching to action."

Power Questions: How can you change the story you tell

yourself so that you focus on benefits for the other person? How can you feel good about your efforts to help someone?

Keep Searching

What is one crucial way to create good luck? Aim for something and take action.

I have had many lucky breaks because I was aiming for something. One of my screenplays was passed from one software engineer to another, then to a real estate developer, and finally to the California Motion Picture Commissioner. Three years later, the same Commissioner secured the San Luis Obispo Airport and an American Eagle airplane—for free—for a motion picture I was directing. (The finished film went to the Cannes Film Festival market.) This lucky break happened because I was searching for help and connections in the film industry. So keep searching for better ways.

Without heroes, we are all plain people, and don't know how far we can go. – Bernard Malamud

The principle is to keep searching and be open to all positive possibilities. Then you will find what you're looking for. Make your dreams come true. "Knowing what you know now, what would you have done differently?" I asked Marcia Wieder, best-selling author of *Making Your Dreams Come True*.

Marcia replied, "I would have done more research about expanding the multimedia creative services agency I had ... I expanded too fast. I didn't really have a full understanding of what that meant in terms of time, effort and commitment. Based on the things I really value like flexibility, freedom and friendship—the two just didn't line up."

Marcia had lived in Washington, DC for 10 years and was president of a company employing up to 15 people. Although she appeared successful, she was not passionate about her work, her clientele and where she lived.

Then she envisioned a new dream, in which she was free to travel anywhere at anytime, live with a view of water and mountains, create her work as play, and live a life filled with self-expression. She moved to San Francisco and started a whole new life. Marcia now says, "I've become a successful dream coach, speaker and author. I have been paid to travel to Hawaii, Rome, Greece, and Indonesia to inspire people to dream."

"What's the best question that anyone ever asked you, and how did you respond?" I asked.

Marcia replied, "On her television show, Oprah asked me what my dream was—after I asked her first. She said her dream was to create a company where people could have fun. And then she asked me, 'What's your dream?' I said, 'My dream is that people will have dreams. That we will open our calendars and schedule the date that we're going to do them.'"

(Marcia Wieder is the author of *Dream* and founder of Dream Coach University, marciawieder.com)

While you keep searching, it is important to discover how to improve your job performance. Use questions that help you focus on career-enhancing actions.

Many of us hold positions that require us to work on multiple projects at one time. The following section outlines a process you can use to identify the vital elements in each project.

1. *Ask your supervisor what she feels is crucial to the success of the project.* Knowing the crucial details (your supervisor's preferences) will help you perform to her expectations.

2. *Ask your supervisor what excellent outcomes she wants from the completion of the project.* When you know what outcomes your supervisor wants, you have more possibilities to meet

and perhaps exceed her expectations.

3. *Ask your supervisor what can be left out of the project.* There is rarely enough time to make everything perfect. However, you can excel on the tasks that your supervisor feels are important. To do this, you must know what she feels can be left out of the project. One of the worst things is to hear your supervisor say, "That's nice, but it really doesn't matter." Asking a question about what can be left out helps you avoid sweating the small stuff.

4. *Send a confirming e-mail.* It's important to discover whether you clearly understand your supervisor's priorities. Some supervisors like e-mail, others do not. Discover your supervisor's preferences. If she is okay with e-mail, follow up on your discussion with a confirming e-mail. If your supervisor does not like e-mail, take good notes and then ask follow-up questions.

5. *Briefly ask, "Did I leave anything out of the e-mail?"* If you use e-mail, make sure to ask this question. This is an opportunity to help your supervisor elaborate on what she really needs you to do.

6. *Ask your supervisor what she feels are your strengths.* It's helpful to know what your supervisor feels you are doing right.

7. *Ask your supervisor what specific steps she thinks you should take to capitalize on your strengths.* Your supervisor's specific instructions will give you a road map to a great performance evaluation.

8. *Ask your supervisor what steps you could de-emphasize, so that you can concentrate on your strengths.* This can help your supervisor expand her awareness so that she'll be able to direct you in ways that provide more value for the company.

9. *Ask your supervisor what skills she feels you need to refine.* This is a hard question for many of us. We'd rather not hear

bad news. However, find out early. Then you can take action toward creating a great performance review. If you wait until review time, it could be too late.

10. *Ask your supervisor what specific steps she'd like you to take toward improving your skills and earning a great performance evaluation.* You can follow up with questions like, "And if I do these steps, I'll earn a five on my next evaluation in the initiative category?"

11. *Listen to your supervisor's speech patterns.* To discover what's important to your supervisor, listen to her speech patterns. In another section of this book, I discuss the four personality styles: Lion, Beaver, Dog, and Peacock. Here is how you can spot each one:

a) **The Lion** (hard-charger) says, "What's the bottom-line here?" "What's taking so long?" "Spare me the details. What's the point?"

b) **The Beaver** (engineer type) says, "Can I be available for a cup of coffee after work? Well, that depends on the Acme account, Joe's letter on the widget issue, Susan's laryngitis, Cindy's..."

c) **The Dog** (relater) says, "Well ... I ... I just ... well, they're pressuring me into a decision on this and I ..."

d) **The Peacock** (socializer) says, "The answer is yes. No, I don't need more data. I've got a feeling about this one. We're going to look good with this one."

Note some of your supervisor's favorite phrases. What personality type do they imply? When you know your supervisor's personality style, you can communicate in ways that help her feel good about you and your work. (For more information on this topic, see the later section entitled *Emphasize Personality Styles*.)

12. *Ask your supervisor, "Ideally, what would you like to see happen?"* Sometimes, supervisors are not sure what they

really want to see happen. This question helps you and your supervisor discover the ideal outcomes to the project. When you can help the desired outcomes occur, you demonstrate your value. Consider using a question like, "Ideally, what would you like to see happen with this project?"

13. *Ask, "How can I better serve (the team, the project, what you're doing ...)?"* This question helps you get to the point. You're asking your supervisor exactly how you can do better. In your journal, write this question in a form you'd be comfortable with, perhaps something like, "How can I better serve the project?"

14. *After your supervisor responds to a question, ask a confirming question.* For example, once I asked a team leader, "Mirnah, what's the next thing you need me to do for the team?" She replied, "Write an article for Acme magazine." Then I reflected on our other deadlines and asked a confirming question: "Oh, so you'd like me to make writing that article my first priority?" Then Mirnah was free to clarify what she preferred me to focus on. In your personal journal, write a confirming question.

Remember to ask questions that clarify your supervisor's expectations. Take notes based on her answers. Finally, follow up to understand your supervisor's expectations.

To form your team, keep searching for people who have similar goals and a similar commitment to excellence.

"[Composer] John Williams has made the biggest contribution to my movies, and they reach the heart universally, in every country, on every continent of this planet. John Williams speaks to people. And John rewrites my movies musically. At the end [of ET, the Extraterrestrial] ILM and I can make those bicycles lift off the ground. We can do that. But John Williams is the only one who can make them truly airborne. Because the audience lifts off the ground on John Williams' violins." – Steven Spielberg

When an entrepreneur hits a plateau, it often means that it's time to expand his or her personal network of contacts. Find ways to be helpful to others, and gently let people know what you do. My client Tarena said to her acquaintance, "You're welcome. I was glad to find that lead for you. Oh, speaking of leads, please let me know if you know someone who is seeking to gain clients quickly. That's my specialty as a sales coach. Thanks."

Principle: Identify what you truly want and keep searching for ways to make it happen.

Power Questions: What do you truly want? First, what do you want to eliminate in your current life? What don't you like about your current life? Now turn it around. (Example: If you don't like your current boring job, the turn-around is, "I want meaningful work that I enjoy.")

Excel on Another Horse

When the horse my father was riding ran straight for the barn, my father had one idea: survive! Good thing, too, because if he hadn't ducked, his head would have slammed into the barn door frame. We often hear the phrase, "Get back on the horse," but my father realized that this errant horse was stuck in its mood. Instead of getting back on that unruly horse, he chose to ride a different horse.

Similarly, years ago I learned to excel on another horse. At that time, as a result of seeing my demo reel, an international seminar company invited me to fly to another state to audition as a speaker. The company was paying for the ticket, so I said, "Sure!" At the audition, I saw two other hopefuls, one of them a young blonde woman who seemed to glow.

Later, the company informed me that I had not been selected. I was extremely disappointed. It was as if I had fallen off a horse. *So I decided to get on another horse:* I rented a space and held my own seminar.

Before this, the seminar company had had control of the decision-making. This time, I took control and created my own opportunity. I made my luck with another horse.

To achieve our goals, we often need to be flexible and select a new method. Earl Nightingale, bestselling author and cofounder of Nightingale-Conant, the leading educational audio program company in the world, said, "Success is the progressive realization of worthy goals." Everyone feels moments of happiness when they achieve a goal or fulfill a desire, but many of us find joyful moments simply by traveling in the direction of our personal goals.

Happiness is how you travel. The crucial thing is to feel happy on the path. We experience more time on the path than at the lofty plateaus of successfully completed projects. When we have methods to experience joy in small daily achievements, we feel better and are more productive.

To experience happiness, it helps to know what is important to you. For example, when Johnny Carson interviewed Jimmy Stewart, star of the Holiday Season movie favorite *It's a Wonderful Life*, Johnny asked, "How would you like to be remembered?" Jimmy thought for a moment and replied, "[As] a guy who believed in hard work and decent values and love of country, love of family, love of community, love of God."

It comes down to the story you tell yourself.
– *Tom Marcoux*

My client Carol was telling herself a story that made her feel bad about a failed project. With my coaching, Carol learned to tell herself a new version of the story: "With this project, I had three goals: (a) serve people, (b) help our careers, and (c) make money. I got two out of three. That was good. And I'm learning how to do better next time."

The detail that helps you excel on another horse

Lynda Obst, producer of *Contact,* starring Jodie Foster, and *Sleepless in Seattle,* starring Tom Hanks and Meg Ryan, was telling me about the early days of her film-industry career, when she used to wear a good-luck outfit to every meeting. I then asked, "What brings you fulfillment?"

She replied, "Writing." This is a crucial detail: if you know what brings you fulfillment, you can be flexible and excel on another horse.

Dr. Bernie Siegel, bestselling author of *Love, Medicine and Miracles,* reported a list of steps for healing and staying well, as written by Steven James. Here are a few of Steven's suggestions:

"Do things that bring a sense of fulfillment, joy and purpose that validate your worth ... Take care of yourself—nourishing, supporting and encouraging yourself ... Release all negative emotions, resentment, envy, sadness, anger. Express your feelings appropriately. Don't hold onto them. Forgive yourself ... Accept yourself and everything in your life as an opportunity for growth and learning. Be grateful. When you screw up, forgive yourself. Learn what you can from the experience and move on ... And keep a sense of humor." – Steven James

To excel on another horse:

1. Observe what is *not* working.

2. Reconnect with your real goal (what brings you fulfillment).

3. Seek another method ("another horse").

4. Take a new action.

Principle: Be observant and discover if you would do better on another horse.

Power Question: What are your criteria to decide if it is better to cut your losses and choose another horse (a more viable opportunity)?

Look to Help

You will get all you want in life if you help enough other people get what they want. – Zig Ziglar

I often ask friends and colleagues, "How can I be supportive of what you're doing?" Once, a video producer responded, "I'm looking for Human Resources managers to participate in a video program." I went to my database of colleagues and connected her with a manager. The video producer later turned around and connected me with an association that engaged me as a speaker. This new speaking lead was a lucky break, which began with my act of kindness.

Make your luck by sowing seeds of help for many people. Some people hesitate to ask if someone needs help. This hesitation arises from fear that the person will ask for too much. The solution is to have prepared responses that follow your offer, so if someone accepts your offer and asks for help, you can give yourself time to think ("think-space"). You can respond, "Hmmm. Let me think about that one. I might be able to connect you with someone who can do that better than I can."

The value of connection is so great that it is worth the effort of asking people what they need. There are hidden pearls of luck waiting for you. You can discover them by helping others.

Great communicators are visible in helping the team effort. Look for ways to help a team effort, and unexpected benefits result. Tom Hanks, wanting the feature film *Saving Private Ryan* to be excellent, suggested that one-third of his own lines be cut. "That's the first time I ever saw an actor cut his own lines," Steven Spielberg said.

Even from the beginning of the production of *Saving Private Ryan,* Tom Hanks was helpful. A crisis arose when Tom and the other actors were in boot camp to train for the film, while Steven Spielberg was busy editing *The Lost World: Jurassic Park II.* Tom called Steven and told him with concern that the actors were fading under the training and they all wanted to quit. Steven said, "Tom, I'm here, and you're there. See what you can do." Tom went back to the other actors, encouraged them and lifted their spirits. The actors stayed with the film. Tom demonstrated that he was a great team player.

Steven trusts Tom. In fact, they later teamed up to co-produce the $120 million HBO mini-series *Band of Brothers,* whose fifth episode was directed by Tom. Connections of trust with others create opportunities.

I love what I do for a living, it's the greatest job in the world, but you have to survive an awful lot of attention that you don't truly deserve and you have to live up to your professional responsibilities and I'm always trying to balance that with what is really important. – Tom Hanks

Principle: Seek to be helpful as your approach to new people, and your opportunities will multiply.

Power Questions: Would you feel comfortable asking, "How can I be supportive of what you're doing?" (If you are hesitating, how would you rephrase this question so that you can ask more easily?)

Use Everything for Networking
Move out of your comfort zone. You can only grow if you are willing to feel awkward and uncomfortable when you try something new. – Brian Tracy

"Are you going to call that person back?" I asked a business owner when I happened to visit while he was playing back a message on his answering machine.

"No," he replied—because the caller had dialed a wrong number. But the business owner could have called back and informed the caller that she needed to try a different phone number. That would have been a kind gesture. Unfortunately, this business owner didn't realize ...

You make your luck by honoring every gift of connection that the universe offers. – Tom Marcoux

Every person we meet can connect us with others. Help people as they appear in your life. You never know when a seed of kindness you plant will later blossom into an opportunity.

Don't be the smartest one in your group. Get a bigger circle ... You have to have people who inspire you, who are further along than you. – Joel Osteen

How to respond to a request for feedback

Sometimes, a person in our network requests feedback. This can be a minefield. A fumble here can create an enemy. First, realize that a number of people asking for a critique are really hoping for your agreement. Here is a process to help you provide nurturing feedback when someone truly asks for your opinion:

1. Ask these questions in this order:

a) Who is it for?

b) What were you aiming for?

c) What were you hoping I'd talk about?

2. Start talking about "what works." (Talk about the elements of the project that are praiseworthy).

3. If the person insists that she wants help to make improvements, ask: "Is there an area you're concerned about?"

4. If possible, refer to a "straw person." Here's an example: "I was wondering how an typical person (in X target market) will compare your DVD's cover with the other DVDs in this genre on Amazon.com" (By referring to the "typical person" you are speaking of a "straw person," that is, a fictional person.)

5. Close your comments with a summary of the praise-worthy elements of the project.

I prefer to talk about "What works ... and Areas to Improve." And I tend to *avoid* the label, *critique.*

Avoid gushing advice. In fact, don't offer unsolicited advice. People's ears will be closed. And if you are pressed to give feedback to someone in your network, make sure that the process is truly a supportive dialogue.

Principle: Welcome surprise opportunities to expand your circle of contacts. Be gracious to everyone.

Power Questions: What are unusual (and safe) ways to meet new people? Can a return call be a possible opening to expand your circle of contacts?

Course-Correct Constantly

Did you know that on any airplane flight bound for Hawaii, the plane is off course about 90% of the time? How does the pilot ensure that you arrive safely and on time? She has the plane make constant adjustments; that is, she course-corrects constantly.

How do you know if you're on target? You put in an evaluation process. A new screenwriter can make sure that her work is reviewed by seasoned screenwriters who have sold screenplays. The new screenwriter does not need to implement all their suggestions, but their input gives her tools for improvement. One idea can spark the crucial idea that makes your project outstanding.

The author Steve Alten sold his used car to gain funds so that he could hire an excellent editor for his first book, *Meg.*

With the editor's revisions, *Meg* attracted a publisher and proved successful. Steve Alten went on to write many novels that have been published.

You get what you inspect. Develop ways of monitoring your progress. This allows you to identify what to continue doing and what to modify.

Course-Correct through Choice-Market Testing™

Imagine that you are considering creating a new product. So many choices arise. How would you pick a catchy title or hook (one-line description)? How would you choose attractive packaging?

To market test a title, use my process of *Choice-Market Testing*. For example, for a film I was producing and directing, I had two poster concepts created.

Then I asked people, "Which movie would you pay to see?" It's crucial to give people a choice, because many prefer to be polite and thus avoid providing critical feedback. If you show them only one cover or title, they say, "That's nice." For real feedback, I always give two choices. I ask, "I have two titles for my new book. If you were on Amazon.com, looking for a book for yourself or a friend, which title would you buy?" I watch their faces. They pause and give a useful answer. Then I gently ask, "I see that you prefer title number two. What do you think that title is about? What about it grabs your interest?" In your personal journal, note two items that can serve for your first use of *Choice-Market Testing*.

Course-Correcting is vital at work. Let's look at three methods to help you protect your job and earn raises:

1. Get credit with progress reports
2. Perform high-visibility tasks
3. Do what you were hired to do

Method 1: Get credit with progress reports

Discover your supervisor's preferences. Once I was hired to be part of a major organization's team. I needed to understand quickly which methods of staying in contact my new supervisor preferred. I asked his assistant, who informed me, "He hardly looks at e-mail. Voicemail is good, but he gets so many calls that he is slow to return them. But he does look at his faxes." Later, I followed up by asking my supervisor directly how he preferred that I stay in contact. When I had some time-urgent information, I left a voicemail message and also sent a fax.

Be effective and help others (including your supervisor) see that you are doing a great job. Get credit for everything you do right. Use your day planner like a job diary. Note all achievements daily so that you can send periodic progress reports to your supervisor. It helps to ask your supervisor, "Would you like me to keep you posted via e-mail?" If she says no, you can give verbal reports and keep notes in your job diary.

Here is a progress report e-mail message:

From: Michelle

To: Nadia

Re: Progress Report

Nadia,

Just to keep you posted. On September 2nd, I began telemarketing with 20 minutes of phone calls each day. To date I have acquired 10 new customers.

Keep all progress reports and e-mails praising your work in a progress file. Bring this file and a summary memo with you when you go in for your review and when you ask for a raise. It is easier to get a raise when you demonstrate that you are a valuable employee.

Lou Heckler, a national speaker and former executive for

ABC television, mentions that he found exact quotes from his own written progress reports (submitted as e-mail messages) in the performance evaluation his supervisor wrote. Lou's supervisor only knew of Lou's actions based on Lou's reports; so in essence, Lou had written his own performance evaluation!

In your personal journal, note specific facts and figures that you can put in your progress report.

Method 2: Perform high-visibility tasks

High-visibility tasks help you do a great job, and they help others see that you're doing well for the company.

Which tasks will make you look good? Jennifer focuses on having her weekly sales figures done one day early, and routinely sending new invoices out in email on the same day.

Which tasks will cause trouble if any errors occur? Jennifer makes sure that all dollar amounts on invoices are accurate and all collection letters are sent at specific intervals (noted in her day planner). These items are vital because if any errors were present, customer complaint letters would go to Jennifer's supervisor. Jennifer devotes significant attention and time to these tasks and protects her job.

In your personal journal, note high-visibility tasks that help you do a great job and help others see your progress. List high-visibility tasks that need to be done carefully.

Method 3: Do what you were hired to do

Remember, your job description is likely to evolve over time, so you need to take time frequently to review which tasks are the most important for you to accomplish. It also helps to have a meeting with your supervisor to clarify the current priorities for your position, taking into account your supervisor's priorities, the good of the department, and the company's mission and objectives.

In your personal journal, write notes on these topics:

a) I was hired to do these specific tasks …

b) Am I completing these tasks efficiently and effectively? If not, how can I improve?

By reviewing these tasks, you are preparing yourself to excel at your job. Remember to focus on high-visibility tasks.

Principle: Make course-corrections constantly.

Power Question: How can you monitor your progress so you can correct your course?

Keep Going for What You Really Want

Once you make a decision, the universe conspires to make it happen. – Ralph Waldo Emerson

Identify what you really want, and the universe moves to help you. Sylvester Stallone was certain that he wanted to portray a boxer in the film *Rocky*, based on his own screenplay.

Early in my acting career I realized the only way I would ever prove myself was to create my own role in my own script. On my 29th birthday, I had $106 in the bank. My best birthday present was a sudden revelation that I had to write the kind of screenplay that I personally enjoyed seeing. I relished stories of heroism, great love, dignity, and courage, dramas of people rising above their stations, taking life by the throat and not letting go until they succeeded … To cheer myself up, I took the last of my entertainment money and went to see the Ali–Wepner fight on closed circuit TV. Chuck Wepner, a battling, bruising club fighter who had never made the big time, was having his shot. It wasn't at all regarded as a serious battle. But as the fight progressed, this miracle unfolded. He hung in there. People went absolutely crazy. Wepner was knocked out in the 15th and final round, almost

lasting the distance. We had witnessed an incredible triumph of the human spirit and we loved it. That night, Rocky Balboa was born.
– Sylvester Stallone

The producer offered Stallone $130,000 if he would just accept a screenwriting fee and give up his desire to act in the film. Stallone had been living at a subsistence level for years, and the offer was incredibly tempting. But Stallone decided to go for what he really wanted: to perform the lead role. He emphasized his true desire, and his attorney made sure the contract contained a clause requiring that if Stallone needed to be removed as lead actor, it couldn't happen until midway through the filming. This strategy was highly effective because the producers would be reluctant to throw away half their production budget and start over.

It was Stallone's clarity of purpose that led to his lucky break. The role of Rocky turned him into a box office superstar and led to four sequels. After the disappointment of *Rocky V*, Stallone wanted to do another film. Six years went by …

The people in the studios that really green light films today are Marketing Department people … Can they sell the film of a 59 year old has-been boxer? Doesn't exactly inspire confidence … But you know what? I said, 'Everyone feels like a has-been when they are not. That is the whole point. That is the whole premise of the story. That we all still have this thing burning inside of us and if we nurture it, it can revitalize us.' This time it almost didn't happen. It was almost an accident. They had turned it down for nearly seven years and then the studio head was replaced. The new studio head happened to walk into a small Mexican restaurant at a few minutes to midnight on New Years Eve in Mexico when he bumped into me at a table. 'Hi Sylvester, how're you doing?' 'Oh, hi Joe. I'm finishing up Rocky Balboa.' 'Can I see it?' … [The new studio head] takes it home. His wife reads it—she cries and the movie was green-lit. So don't ever underestimate women in boxing. - Sylvester Stallone

Finally, in 2006, when Stallone was 59 years old—thirty years after the first Rocky film—he wrote and directed *Rocky Balboa*. It proved to be a critical and commercial success.

Never give up. And never stop believing.

- tag line for the film Rocky Balboa

Whoopi Goldberg has also demonstrated the power of persistence. She dealt with dyslexia and supported herself by working as a bricklayer and a funeral parlor make-up artist. (By the way, both Sean Connery and Jackie Chan also supported themselves for a time as bricklayers.)

Eventually, Whoopi created a one-woman satirical production in which she played several characters. Her show originated in San Francisco and toured the U.S. and Europe. The show earned acclaim and the attention of director Mike Nichols. Mike directed a 1984 Broadway version of the show, which earned Whoopi a Drama Desk Award and Theatre World Award, as well as a Grammy for the album recording.

Whoopi's breakthrough in film came when she portrayed the lead character in Steven Spielberg's movie of the Alice Walker novel, *The Color Purple*. Whoopi's performance was rewarded with an Oscar nomination and Best Actress Golden Globe, providing the actress with instant stardom. Then it looked as though Whoopi made some big mistakes. She had a number of roles in movies that were box office duds.

I don't believe that there is any "good career move" or "bad career move." I believe there are only the things that make me happy. – Whoopi Goldberg

I am where I am because I believe in all possibilities ... I am the American Dream. I am the epitome of what the American Dream basically said. It said, you could come from anywhere and be anything you want in this country. That's exactly what I've done.

– *Whoopi Goldberg*

Principle: Keep going for what you really want.

Power Questions: What would you do if Aladdin's kind genie offered you exactly what you truly desire—if you only wrote it down? Another version: If you knew that you could not fail, what would you do? What is your pie-in-the-sky desire?

Part X
Great Communicators Give
Compelling Speeches

What would you do if you were terrified of speaking before a group? Would you become a professional speaker? That's what I did.

How did I make the transition? When I was in grammar school, I was pushed to play the piano for thirty-one elderly people living in a senior-care facility. I sat down and my leg began to shake. I was sure they could see my terror. My foot shook so hard that I was afraid it would fall off the pedal with an embarrassing *thud*. I was focused on the thoughts, "How am I doing? They've heard these songs before. My playing is not that good. They'll wince at all the wrong notes."

My fear of public performance has been part of my path to being a public speaker who entertains thousands of people all across the United States. I had to learn techniques to handle my fears. When I speak now, my focus is, "How may I serve?" I let go of the thought, "How am I doing?"

To make things better, it is crucial that you take action. To give good speeches, here's my action: I rehearse. Anytime I feel uneasy about an upcoming speech, I rehearse for a few moments.

Jay Conrad Levinson shares similar insights about taking action:

Instantly
by Jay Conrad Levinson

I make tough situations better by eliminating them ASAP each time. One of life's greatest satisfactions for me seems to be throwing things away. Although you'd never know it to look around my home, I seem to be dedicated to removing stuff from my files, computer desktop, real desktop, in-basket, and to-do list. At the end of every workday, which means Monday through Wednesday to me, I delight in crossing the final task off the list in my datebook.

At the end of every year, I cross the line into true ecstasy when I fill several full-sized garbage cans with paper no longer needed. I feel pretty much the same when I relieve my hard drive of data nobody on earth will ever need again. I've learned that by dealing with work assignments only one time, I am able to gain a lot more precious free time for myself. Instead of putting the work aside for a later date, I deal with it at the moment it comes in, so that I won't have to be involved with it ever again. People say that I'm a good e-mail correspondent. I answer that it's mainly because I don't like having e-mail to answer. That's why I'm getting back to you instantly.

Jay Conrad Levinson was the author of the bestselling marketing series in history, *Guerrilla Marketing*, plus 56 other business books. His books have sold over 21 million copies worldwide. And his guerrilla concepts have influenced marketing so much that his books appear in 43 languages and are required reading in MBA programs worldwide.

If you are called on to give a speech, it helps to follow Jay's example and take action instantly—that is, rehearse.

If you are confronted with the situation of needing to give a speech within one week, or even within five minutes, you can use the following S.P.E.E.C.H. process:

S – Summarize

P – Prepare your first sentence and last sentence

E – Express an anecdote

E – Enter with a benefit

C – Conclude with "Thank you"

H – Honor three memorable points

Summarize

What is the most important point, which you want your audience to remember for weeks after your speech?

Imagine how great you would feel if someone came up to you one year later and said, "I heard your speech, and I will always remember that you said … " This is what happened for speaker/author Hyrum Smith, CEO and cofounder of Franklin Quest Company (prior to a later merger). Hyrum gave a speech, and one year later he received this letter:

Hyrum, I went to your seminar a year ago in Princeton. It

never occurred to me that what I do on a daily basis ought to be based on my governing values ... the things that really matter most to me ... I decided to dedicate my life to making a good life for my son [here he describes several activities shared with his son] ... Hyrum, last week my son, eight years old, was killed in an automobile accident. I have experienced some real pain at the loss of my son. But I have to tell you that I have experienced no guilt ... Hyrum, thank you.

Inspired by Hyrum's speech, this father had taken action to make a good life for his son. To make a powerful impact such as this, we must know our most important point. That point will be a highlight of the summary at the end of the speech.

Your summary creates the powerful ending you desire. I emphasize to my clients that a good speech ends with the speaker in control. Avoid ending with a question-and-answer period. A Q&A session has a puttering-out effect.

Instead, prepare for your ending by writing down three memorable points. At the end of your speech, say something like: "And now I will summarize. First, remember to ... Second, we do better when we ... And finally, you make a great impact by ... Thank you."

Speak properly, and in as few words as you can, but always plainly; for the end of speech is not ostentation, but to be understood. – William Penn

A proverb is much matter distilled into few words.
– Buckminster Fuller

Do not say a little in many words, but a great deal in a few.
– Pythagoras

Principle: End with strength. Summarize your points.

Power Question: What are your three main points? Write down a strong way to repeat those points in a summary.

Prepare Your First Sentence and Your Last Sentence

Did you ever attend a speech that the speaker simply read? Have you endured watching a speaker stare at the back wall as he spoke, as if his speech was plastered on that wall?

I advise my graduate students to avoid memorizing each word of a speech. Instead, we want the presentation to have a rapport-creating naturalness. It helps to start strongly with a memorized first sentence and end powerfully with a memorized last sentence.

For your first sentence, you can begin with:

- A question
- A powerful fact
- A detail that moves emotions

Be sincere; be brief; be seated. - President Franklin D. Roosevelt

Principle: People remember the beginning and end of your speech. Start and finish with strength.

Power Questions: What is a strong first sentence for your speech? Note three possibilities. What is a memorable last sentence for your speech? Note three possibilities.

Express an Anecdote

How do you get past a person's natural resistance? Tell a story. Here we will designate an anecdote as a "story with a point." In fact, a powerful way to state clearly the value of a story is to end it with "And so, my point is ..." or to conclude with "What I learned that day was ... "

What we observe is not nature itself, but nature exposed to our method of questioning. – Werner Heisenberg (physicist)

Related to Heisenberg's comment, we see that our story is like a "method of questioning." When questioning something we are actually forming our own version of a story. Choose your questions well to set the direction of your story. The anecdote touches the hearts of your audience in ways that logic and rational arguments cannot.

We're not seeing what's real; we just see our story.

– Tom Marcoux

A good, heartfelt story helps you give the audience a new view of reality. The story provides an experience in which the audience can invest their emotions. Carefully select three anecdotes and try them with friends and family. Find out which anecdote reaches people's hearts.

Principle: Express an anecdote to seize attention and change lives.

Power Question: How can you make your point with an anecdote that inspires minds and moves emotions?

Enter with a Benefit

"Would you like me to show you how to have an extra $364 for your next vacation with no work, ethically and legally?"* Our ears and thoughts tend to be tuned to: "What's in it for me?" So begin with a benefit for the listener.

(* At one point, I placed the minimal down payment to hold a reservation at a resort. Then, I placed the balance of vacation savings in a Certificate of Deposit account to earn interest.)

Another way to begin a speech is, "Imagine if I could show you how to make $1,000 a minute in a job interview. That's what we're going to discuss today."

When you start a speech, the listener subconsciously asks the Three Ws:

1. Who are you?
2. Why should I listen to you?
3. What's in it for me?

Answer these questions. You seize the listeners' attention and are on the path to be heard and be trusted.

Researchers report that people will put out more effort to

avoid a loss than to gain joy. When addressing a workshop audience, I illustrated this point by placing a $10 bill on my left knee and a $20 bill on my right knee. I mimed having the $10 snatched away. I then asked, "What will people put more effort into, avoiding the loss of $10 or gaining $20?" The attendees replied, "Not losing the $10." They were correct. Audience members told me that this illustration makes a visceral impact, driving home the point that we're all interested in avoiding loss.

Hard-charging people are concerned about the loss of time. They fear things that "waste their time."

Focus on being productive rather than being busy—your life depends on it. – Timothy Ferris

Show people how they will save time, gain leverage, and get more done, and you have their attention. When you focus your speech on the vital few, your audience will bless you. By "the vital few," I mean the three major points that provide compelling benefits for your audience. I emphasize three benefits because that gives you three chances that any given audience member will find one of the benefits to be compelling.

Place benefits in your pitch. A pitch is a brief presentation usually designed to get someone (in the film or publishing industry) to read something. A pitch is also used in sales.

The idea of putting a benefit into your pitch is to give the listener an experience of the benefit you're offering.

When I guide my clients in the art of pitching, I include these ideas to improve the pitch:

1. Avoid beginning with the best idea.

2. Warm them up.

3. Often, you can begin by explaining how you came up with the idea.

4. Introduce suspense (tension, suspense and release).

5. End in a big, memorable way.

6. Ask for the order. ("And so, I hope you will say yes to publishing my book.")

If you are pitching a screenplay or novel, the benefit you're giving is the experience of anticipation or curiosity. That's the reason I said "introduce suspense." Your target is to get the listener to feel, "This story has potential. I wonder how it works out!"

Ask for the order. To ask for the order is to request clearly and gently what you want. For your closing, use this pattern: "Because of (first reason) and (second reason), I encourage you to please say *yes* to my project."

By providing two powerful reasons for saying *yes*, you are guiding the listener to respond favorably. Also, by saying the word *yes*, you have put the idea of *yes* into the room. Then yes will echo in the thoughts of the decision-makers.

Principle: Begin with a benefit.

Power Questions: What is the most compelling benefit that you offer with your speech? How will you make the audience members' lives better, easier, more profitable or more fulfilling?

Conclude with "Thank You"

Imagine you have just heard one of the most inspiring speeches in your life. Your blood is pumping. You feel a zing of energy. You know in your heart that amazing possibilities are in store for you. Then the speech ends with "That's it," like a deflated balloon.

One of the best speakers I have heard ends her speeches with "That's it," smiling and rocking back on her heels. This deflates the life-changing, uplifting power of her message.

On the other hand, a great communicator pauses after her

final statement and simply says, "Thank you." Those are two powerful words. You have just participated in something important. You and the audience have had a dialogue, even if you did all the talking and they did the nodding. They gave you their attention. You gave them words to grow on.

Helen Keller said something that truly opened my eyes. Scarlet fever in her infancy had left her blind and deaf, and no one thought she would ever be able to talk. Her teacher, Anne Sullivan, helped Helen learn to speak. Helen wrote,

I thank God for my handicaps for, through them, I have found myself, my work, and my God. – Helen Keller

The idea of "thank you" is not merely for the end of the speech. Numerous scholars and authors talk about what you attract in your life.

The enlightened give thanks for what most people take for granted. As you begin to be grateful for what most people take for granted, that vibration of gratitude makes you more receptive to good in your life. – Dr. Michael Bernard Beckwith

What this power is, I cannot say. All I know is that it exists and it becomes available only when you are in that state of mind in which you know exactly what you want. – Alexander Graham Bell

Ask, and it will be given you; Seek, and you will find; Knock, and it will be opened to you. – Jesus of Nazareth

Be thankful toward your audience before you give the speech. Reach out to audience members as they come in the door. I saw top speaker Zig Ziglar shake hands with everyone as they entered an auditorium.

Principle: Conclude your speech with a heartfelt "Thank you."

Power Questions: What are the gifts you are giving with your speech? What can you feel proud of bringing to your audience? (Remember a time when you were grateful for someone's kindness. Focus on that feeling. Then connect with feeling grateful to audience members for their respectful attention.)

Honor Three Memorable Points

What do you remember from the last speech or workshop you attended? Researchers have noted that people tend to remember only about three points from a speech. So choose your points with care. Make them memorable.

If you have an important point to make, don't try to be subtle or clever. Use the pile driver. Hit the point once. Then come back and hit it again. Then hit it a third time—a tremendous whack!

— Winston Churchill

In his speech to a graduating class at Stanford University, Steve Jobs said, "Today I want to tell you three stories from my life. That's it. No big deal. Just three stories. The first story is about connecting the dots."

Later in the speech he said, "… you can't connect the dots looking forward; you can only connect them looking backwards. So you have to trust that the dots will somehow connect in your future. You have to trust in something—your gut, destiny, life, karma, whatever."

Further on in his speech, Steve said, "My third story is about death. When I was 17, I read a quote that went something like, 'If you live each day as if it was your last, someday you'll most certainly be right.' It made an impression on me, and since then, for the past 33 years, I have looked in the mirror every morning and asked myself: 'If today were the last day of my life, would I want to do what I am about to do today?' And whenever the answer has been 'No' for too many days in a row, I know I need to change something."

From these excerpts, you can see how Steve Jobs used structure powerfully and focused on three stories. People remember three points of a speech. When you make sure to have three memorable points, you're on your way to being memorable as a speaker.

Larry King, who hosted CNN's "Larry King Live," described the elements that make someone memorable. He said, "You're a good guest [for my show with] four things:

1. Passion,
2. An ability to explain what [you] do very well,
3. A little bit of a chip on [your] shoulder, and
4. A sense of humor, hopefully self-deprecating."

To explain what you do very well, it helps to form three memorable points. In giving speeches, however, it is often advisable to leave out the chip on the shoulder. And we certainly look for people who have energy and enthusiasm.

As I guide my graduate students to make memorable speeches, I tell them, "What's the big idea? Now add two more." Using three memorable points helps you be clear. Being clear puts you on the path to be heard and be trusted.

Principle: People remember three points of any speech.

Power Question: What are the three most important, life-changing points of your speech? What would make you feel great for the audience to remember?

Part XI
Great Communicators Persuade with Ease

How would your life be better if you could persuade people with ease?

To organize a persuasive speech quickly, it helps to use the P.E.R.S.U.A.D.E. process:

P – Point to the benefit

E – Emphasize personality styles

R – Request a response

S – Say a story

U – Use personal brand (credibility)

A – Ask questions

D – Demonstrate and involve them

E – Energize the emotional brain

The information I share with you is hard won, gained through my own efforts. During one of my first speeches, at seven p.m. on a Friday, a man in the audience actually snored. Scared and concerned, I immediately set forth to become a dynamic speaker who could enthrall audiences. I quickly learned to infuse my speeches with humor and good pacing. Wouldn't you have done the same?

A good scare is worth more to a man than good advice.

– Edgar Watson Howe

Never, ever underestimate the power of "I'd like that."

– John Mayer

Like other professional speakers, I was moved by speeches I'd heard. Listening to an audio program on communication gave me an edge in my business interactions. Later, when I saw a certain speaker, I felt, "Hey! I could do that!"

Now you will learn the skills that will enable you to persuade with ease.

Point to the Benefit

"If I could show you how to become a billionaire in just eight years, would that be of value to you?" I asked my audience. Imagine their rapt attention!*

(* The process of how Ross Perot became a billionaire in only eight years is revealed in my book, Wake Up Your Spirit to Prosperity.*)*

Imagination is everything. It is the preview of life's coming attractions. – Albert Einstein

Engage people's imagination. Have them imagine and see the good outcomes that can occur if they receive your message.

As mentioned earlier, the Three Ws are the audience's subconscious questions:

- Who are you?
- Why should I listen to you?
- What's in it for me?

Answer these Three Ws in your introduction. You can say, "Today I will show you how to make widgets. Then you will enjoy … "

Life will give you what you attract with your thoughts. Think, act, and talk negatively and your world will be negative. Think and act and talk with enthusiasm and you will attract positive results. – Michael LeBoeuf

Mention the benefits at the beginning of your speech and you will capture your audience's attention.

Principle: Begin with compelling benefits.

Power Questions: Where is your audience hurting? How can you take away their pain? What benefits (that your audience is clamoring for) can you offer with your speech?

Emphasize Personality Styles

How do you connect with audience members when something you say can appeal to some and turn off others?

The only thing that will redeem mankind is cooperation.
– Bertrand Russell

The greatest communicators know that diverse individuals listen to their speeches. The idea is to provide various details that appeal to the different personality styles. In essence, you cooperate with each individual's personality style.

A powerful way to make a connection is to use insights related to personality styles. Authors Dr. Tony Alessandra, Michael O'Connor, Nicholas Boothman, and Roger Dawson have discussed personality styles. In what follows, I put my own spin on their research.

Over the years that I have conveyed this material, I have found that using images related to animals makes these insights more memorable. Here is the brief sketch of the four personality styles that I revealed earlier:

Lion: A hard-charging leader, who may be considered abrupt or bossy.

Dog: A supporter, who likes routine and cares about the feelings of others. This person may be slow to accept change.

Peacock: An extrovert, who loves to stand out in a crowd and gain approval. This person may be ineffective when it comes to follow-up.

Beaver: An analytical person, who likes tables, graphs and lots of details. This person wants to appear intelligent, and may make decisions slowly due to a great fear of making a mistake.

Ways you can reach each personality style when speaking

Lion: Write a list of points and check off the completed points as you go through the speech. (You can use a flipchart or computer-based solution.)

Beaver: Write a list of points and check off the completed points as you go through the speech.

Peacock: Talk with the Peacock before your speech. Then, during the speech, say, "Sam had a good idea about pre-screening the applicants. Sam, how about telling the group your idea?" (This gives Sam a chance to "look good.")

Dog: At the beginning of the speech, ask, "What were you hoping and expecting I'd talk about? What topic would help you if I addressed it, so that you'd go home saying, 'I got exactly what I needed from the presentation'?" Listen carefully. Thank each person. Write five or six of the comments on the board and check them off during your speech.

Principle: The greatest communicators provide benefits that appeal to a variety of personality styles.

Power Questions: What personality styles are likely to be represented in your audience? How can you provide benefits customized to each of these personality styles?

Request a Response

How do you keep your audience awake and receptive to your message? Request a response. Many effective speeches are really a form of dialogue. And, just like a good trial attorney, when you are going to request a response, plan in advance the questions whose answers can help you.

The things that get rewarded get done ... People do what gets measured. – Michael LeBoeuf

You need to rehearse so you can smoothly and effectively request a response. In order to make sure that you rehearse, set up a schedule. Even nine minutes a day will help. You can ask five friends if you could rehearse a two-minute section with each. To identify what a good response would be, you need to pre-plan the overall affect of your speech.

My [television] show [Roseanne] showed a family with unconditional love. ... I went through daily battles to reach that goal, and refused to say lines that would humiliate Dan [the husband, portrayed by John Goodman]. Standup [comedy] taught me to author my own work. Standup taught me discipline.

– Roseanne Barr

The point here is, focus on your goal. When you are going to ask for a response, be sure to pre-plan your request so you get the response you're looking for. You, too, can leave your audience with something great.

Principle: Pre-plan the requests for responses that you will use.

Power Questions: What would be the best ways for your audience to respond to your request? What would be okay responses? What would be terrible responses, and how would you recover from them?

Say a Story

How do you avoid stimulating any natural resistance in your listener? Tell a story.

Hearing stories acts as a kind of mental flight simulator, preparing us to respond more quickly and effectively.
– Chip Heath and Dan Heath
My life is my message. – Mahatma Gandhi

The best stories are often ones from your own life. For one thing, the story will be original. When you tell your own story, you have complete credibility and authority. To guide your listeners to realize the benefit, sum up the story with, "What I learned was … "

One of my mentors, international speaker and author Dottie Walters, emphasized the value of stories. Dottie Walters was a master storyteller, who lives on in my heart and in my books. She was my first mentor in the speaking industry. I learned from Dottie the spirit of service that the great speakers embody.

I had the privilege to be coached by Dottie in person a number of times and to interview her for my books, too. When I was with Dottie, she infused me with the confidence that I could do just about anything, that I could rise from where I was, serve people and live abundantly.

For this book, I asked Dottie, "Knowing what you know

now, what would you have done differently?"

"I would have believed in myself and not been so frightened," she replied. She told me about her childhood in a family troubled by domestic violence. Her father's last comment before his final departure from home was, "She's not worth going to college." Dottie told me that his comment was like "knocking a kid down the stairs." Her self-esteem was crushed.

But her mother encouraged Dottie's reading and took her to the public library. There Dottie discovered private coaches, as she read the biographies of Albert Einstein, Joan of Arc, Amelia Earhart, Benjamin Franklin and others. These individuals showed her the way. Dottie would say that Einstein seemed to be telling her, "Dottie, stop focusing on the problem and start concentrating on solutions."

One time, as Dottie was relaying this story to an audience, a woman said, "Who do you think you are? He didn't write that for you!"

Dottie responded, "Didn't he write it for all of us who needed him?"

The truth is that Dottie did rise to believe in herself, and she raised thousands of people up with her. She opened a whole new world for me. Her inspiration led me to expand my journey from motion picture director to communicator and to add to my life, authoring 35 books, speaking in cities across the United States and being a faculty instructor to graduate students and a guest instructor at Stanford University.

Although she passed away on February 14, 2007, Dottie is with me every time I step in front of my audiences and students.

Dottie's rejoinder, "Didn't Albert Einstein write it for all of us who needed him?" reminds me of Mark Twain's comment, "The man who does not read good books has no advantage over the man who cannot read them." Both Dottie and Mark Twain invite to us to continue reading. When we read, we get access to empowering quotes and stories that can enhance our lives.

Principle: An effective story engages the mind, moves the heart and melts resistance.

Power Questions: What are three stories that have moved you the most? What characteristics do these stories have? How can you make sure your story has similar elements?

Use a Personal Brand (Credibility)

My philosophy is that not only are you responsible for your life, but doing the best at this moment puts you in the best place for the next moment. – Oprah Winfrey

As I mentioned earlier, the audience has subconscious questions, the Three Ws:
- Who are you?
- Why should I listen to you?
- What's in it for me?

Answer the Three Ws and you have credibility. Use your personal brand to answer all three questions. Your personal brand is about credibility.

In my books *10 Seconds to Wealth* and *Secrets of Awesome Dinner Guests,* I go into depth about the personal brand. Here I am emphasizing the essence of your personal brand. It's what makes you unique and trustworthy to your listener. Your personal brand is the answer to the question, "What are you best known for?"

A professional is someone who can do his best work when he doesn't feel like it. – Alistair Cooke

All top professionals have devoted significant time and practice to coming up with the few powerful words that convey their competence and trustworthiness.

Sometimes you can borrow credibility. How? You can talk about having interviewed someone who provided special information. For example, when I interviewed Susan RoAnne, bestselling author of *How to Work a Room*, I asked, "Knowing what you know now, what would you have done differently?"

She replied, "When my book was profiled in *USA Today* and *The Wall Street Journal* … I would have tripled my fees."

Be sure to write out your answer to the question, "What are you best known for?" Practice saying the answer, and you're ready to wow a job interviewer or potential customer.

Principle: People listen when the speaker has credibility. The clearly expressed personal brand provides this credibility.

Power Questions: What are you best known for? How can you express your personal brand in ways that inspire audience members to feel they will gain big benefits?

Ask Questions

In my public speaking class, I emphasize, I can't persuade you if I don't know you.

How can you get to know your audience? Ask questions.

Instead of 600 books on the secrets of selling, try this: Ask. Just ask people to buy. Ask, ask, ask, ask, and ask. Become a master asker. – Larry Winget

When you ask your audience questions, you create a rapport. Once rapport is created, you can influence them to accept the value of your ideas.

I'm intensely curious. And I have no agenda … I go in trying to learn. I ask short questions. I leave me out of it. I don't use the word 'I'. – Larry King

Demonstrate that you are interested in your audience's

well-being. Ask gentle questions and listen intently. Ask follow-up questions.

If possible, don't take a stance that is directly opposite to an answer given by an audience member. You can respond, "That's part of it, & the detail we can emphasize now is..." or, "Let's keep that one on the table here..."

It helps to pre-plan some of your questions. For example, I often ask, "How many of us have ever procrastinated on something at some time in our lives?" I raise my hand, and many audience members respond by raising their hands. Some audience members don't.

"Those of you not raising your hands are procrastinating on raising your hands." The audience laughs in response.

First, I have lightened it up. Then I ask a follow-up question: "When you absolutely need to get something done, what breaks your procrastination?"

Often, an audience member will reply, "Fear. For example, I'm afraid of tax penalties." At that point, my audience is fully engaged. Do you see the power of questions?

Asking questions of your audience keeps them engaged. A question-and-answer session can make a powerful impact.

Here are helpful strategies:

1. *Avoid ending your speech with a question-and-answer session.* The greatest communicators regain control of their speeches after the Q&A session and end with a rousing summary. To stay in control, you can say, "In a moment, I will take a few questions. Then I will summarize."

2. *Handle the silence that may happen when you ask, "Any questions?"* You can comment, "That's okay. People are thinking. We'll take a moment here."

3. *If the silence continues, you can say, "Oh, in the meantime, I have a question."* Then state a rhetorical question that relates

to one of the points in your speech, and answer your own question. By doing this, you have given your audience time to formulate their questions.

4. *To end your question-and-answer session, say, "I can take two more questions."* Then continue with, "I can take one question … Now I will summarize."

We have the power to turn a question into a gift—even if it was thrown like a spear. – Tom Marcoux

How to handle tough questions

Sara is giving a presentation aimed at gaining funding for her new company. From the audience of potential investors, a man asks, "How can you expect us to go with you when your previous company went under?"

Sara takes a few steps toward the questioner and replies with composure, "John, I hear your concern. In the five years since my previous company, I have dived into this segment of the industry. My experience as a Vice President at Acme Company showed me how … "

With this response, Sara demonstrates what I call the *Power-Three for Handling Tough Questions*, which I share the with CEOs and my other clients. To make this technique clear, I will break down Sara's response and show how to win the audience over.

1. Catch the question (an aikido blending move).

Sara replies, "John, I hear your concern." In the martial art aikido, one "blends" with the opponent's energy. Sara does not contradict John's question. (Sometimes before an audience, I demonstrate how one catches a question by using a by having someone toss me a book and catching it gently in a pillow.)

2. Answer the question.

Sara makes sure to answer John's question: "In the five

years since my previous company, I have dived into this segment of the industry. My experience as a Vice president at Acme Company showed me how ... " She can continue, "I have learned how to deal with Problem A in this segment of the industry."

3. Shine light on a diamond.

Only after Sara has answered the question does she shine light on what she wants to talk about. In effect, she has earned the right by answering the question. ("Earn the right" is a phrase emphasized by speech coach Jerry Weissman.)

Novice politicians sometimes make the mistake of ignoring a question and jumping right back to their talking points. The audience is too sophisticated for this move. It is better to answer the question. If you do not have the data you need to answer the question at the moment, you can mention this fact.

When you are preparing a speech, remember that you have not finished until you have written the ten worst questions you can receive and two possible answers to each question. Remember, courage is easier when you're prepared.

Network effectively with a high ranking individual

Effective questions can help you when meeting top-level professionals, who can ultimately assist your career, like CEOs, bestselling authors, or producers. You need to pre-plan your questions, so that at any moment when you happen to meet a top-level person or celebrity, you are prepared to ask effective questions.

Remember, top professionals are repeatedly accosted by people who want something from them. Many of them are jaded. Here are tips for when you meet them:

1. Say something specific. When I was talking with a motion picture director at the screening of his new feature film, I said, "You really held the tension in the bank scene. I wanted to yell at the character, 'Don't ruin your life!'"

2. Use the powerful way to give a compliment. Be specific: "I really appreciate how you did … (Specify.) How did you do that?" or "How did you learn to do that?"

3. Ask, "What's next for you?" or "What are you looking forward to?"

4. Be brief and be gone.

Principle: Ask questions and you connect with people's hearts and minds.

Power Questions: Write a list of ten questions. Which of these questions feels most appropriate to you? Which questions touch on what truly bothers your audience members? Then write down at least two answers to 10 tough questions you might receive. (Before giving a speech, you can connect with an insider and learn about the questions that most concern that particular audience. Or you might use a brief questionnaire that you can send through e-mail.)

Demonstrate and Involve Them
I hear and I forget.
I see and I remember.
I do and I understand. – Confucius (Kong Qiu)

In preparing a speech, I thought "How can I get the audience to feel the difference between a destructive reaction and a gentle, blending response?"

In front of the audience, I demonstrated the difference between karate and aikido. I invited one attendee to stand up and had him mime a punch. I showed how much effort was needed to block the punch, karate style; then I showed the gentleness of an aikido move. One shifts position, grabs the arm, and guides the person to the floor. I stopped in time so the guy didn't go all the way to the floor. That would have been awkward.

I did this to illustrate the power of providing feedback that avoids creating resistance. **It's important to realize that getting the audience involved makes your point memorably.** One way to get the audience involved is to have people pair off as two-person "teams."

The power of having audience members partner up is that we often feel better when we can express ourselves and be heard. Secondly, we feel good about ourselves when we help someone by listening and supporting that person.

Helping others makes us feel better. When I met Gerald "Jerry" Jampolsky, MD, bestselling author of *Love is Letting Go of Fear*, I was filled with a great energy. Jerry is so inspired that he practically glows. He teaches that when you help someone, you naturally feel better.

One of Jerry's favorite examples is about two boys, Paul and Tony. At 13 years old, Paul had a brain tumor. At 10, Tony had bone cancer severe enough to necessitate the amputation of his leg. When Tony was in the hospital during the scary and painful treatment, Jerry asked Paul to talk with Tony on the phone.

Paul was suffering, too; he looked almost dead. But Jerry noticed that Paul suddenly came alive when he was telling Tony jokes. As they talked, a close friendship emerged. While Paul was helping Tony, Paul felt better!

Not only did Paul help Tony, but he also inspired 50 million people who saw this story on "60 Minutes." I saw this video segment when Jerry invited me to visit The Center for Attitudinal Healing, which he founded. I went to the Center, in Sausalito, California, to discover how I might help Jerry's work. One of the things I am doing is bringing stories like this to the attention of audiences and readers like you.

Here is the Web site: www.AttitudinalHealing.org.

At this Web site we learn, "At the heart of Attitudinal Healing is the belief in the extraordinary ability of ordinary people to be of help to one another, and the idea that we have the power to choose our attitude in any given moment, regardless of circumstances." Please go to the Web site to learn of the 130 locations worldwide.

It often happens that being hit with some form of loss makes people feel somehow less effective and less complete.

By helping another person, we see and feel that we are still effective and strong enough to make a difference in that person's life. This is powerfully nurturing. This is an affirmation: *I help someone and feel the helping process heal us both.*

Here is how this applies to giving a powerful speech: you help someone when you make the person part of your demonstration. For example, you can place the brochure or product in her hand.

Principle: Demonstrate and involve audience members.

Power Questions: How can you have audience members participate? Can you get them (a) moving, (b) talking with a partner or (c) talking with you directly?

Energize the Emotional Brain

What if you had information that you knew was crucial for the well-being of your audience? What could you do to seize their attention? You could show the audience how to avoid a loss.

Researchers have shown that the emotional brain consists of the amygdala and the brain stem. To energize the emotional brain is to give the listener an experience of the pain that occurs if the listener does not implement your suggestion.

A man who is afraid will do anything. – Jawaharlal Nehru
When love and skill work together, expect a masterpiece.
– John Ruskin

A.L. Williams, author of *All You Can Do Is All You Can Do, But All You Can Do Is Enough!* endured the pain of financial disaster when his father died unexpectedly. Since his father did not have life insurance, William's family was left without financial support. After this extreme experience, Williams became an evangelist for adequate insurance coverage. He combined love and skill. A.L. loved to help people protect themselves and their loved ones from financial disaster.

Your emotion moves the audience's emotions. Your passion for your topic can provide the wind beneath the audience's wings. For example, Danny Glover (star of *Lethal Weapon IV*, with Mel Gibson), said, "First you have to determine whether or not you have a passion for acting. I believe that persistence and passion can overcome anything … Remember that what you do is an act of giving, an act of love. It has to be an act of love… "

Danny also said, "I never really considered art as anything other than a vehicle to move people." Danny reminds us that our passion for something is the source of our strength. He wanted to produce and star in a feature film entitled The Prince of Fort Washington, so he made a deal with the studio. The plan was for Danny to star in another Lethal Weapon movie, and in exchange the studio would advance funds for the motion picture he really wanted to do. Danny combined love and skill. I had the opportunity to meet Danny when he presided over a San Francisco screening of his completed film.

People have four basic preoccupations: self-preservation, romance, money, and recognition. – Roy Garn

To effectively stimulate the buyer's emotional brain, we need to become comfortable about money. For many of us, this is a tall order. Here is a story related to the process of getting comfortable about the issue of money:

The bat felt good in my hands. The ball flew toward me. Thwaaack! My bat connected with the ball, and it soared toward the faraway fence, center field. I was stunned. I had never hit a ball that far. It was going, going, almost out of the park, when ...

Whump! Judy, my fellow camp counselor, caught the ball. Judy and I enjoyed pats on the back from our teammates and gave each other a hug. Minutes later, we received simple awards: Best Slugger and Best Catch.

The game and the bat in my hands were tools to bring the camp counselors closer together in our shared vision of enriching the lives of the children in our care. On that day, I used the bat as a tool for goodness and closeness. However, you sometimes hear of someone using a bat for an inappropriate, violent purpose.

The bat and, yes, money are neutral tools. It is time that we become comfortable with how we relate to money.

Comfort about money ties in with the emotional brain.

Lots of us have been conditioned to feel bad about money, as if having money makes one less—less spiritual, for example. If you feel bad about money, you won't be strong enough to use all the tools you need, such as stimulating a potential buyer's emotional brain. Remember, the emotional brain is focused on feelings of loss.

An interviewer asked, "Why would someone be unlikely to stimulate the buyer's emotional brain?"

I replied, "Let me give you a specific example. Joe is a novice salesperson. If he feels bad about money, he will be reluctant to be in that pain. That will make him hesitate to make the potential buyer feel bad, too. It is as if Joe tells himself subconsciously, 'I'm a bad person to focus on gaining money. And I'm a worse person to make the potential buyer feel bad temporarily.'"

The interviewer then asked, "Why is Joe making the buyer feel bad temporarily?"

"Because sometimes, someone won't buy a thing that is good for him until he feels how he could be hurt by not having the product," I replied.

Again, A. L. Williams helped people imagine the pain of the financial disaster that would ensue if one died without adequate life insurance coverage. Only when his customer could imagine a painful consequence did the person buy insurance.

Make gaining financial abundance a positive path. Many top achievers and millionaires have discovered ways to help people on a significant scale. Financial abundance then arrives as a by-product.

Peter McWilliams, author of *Wealth 101*, notes that wealth refers to "health, happiness, abundance, prosperity, riches, loving, caring, sharing, learning, knowing what you want, opportunity, enjoying and balance." A spiritual view of wealth includes being grateful for the blessings we currently enjoy, and being comfortable with the idea of going for more. You can see that we can have both.

Film provides an opportunity to marry the power of ideas with the power of images. – Steven Bochco

As in film, when giving a persuasive speech we can combine the power of ideas and images. Express a word picture and you inspire an image in the listeners' minds.

Here is an example of a word picture that I mentioned earlier: "When I'm waiting for you, I'm like a puppy on a raft in the middle of the Atlantic Ocean, not knowing if a rescue boat will ever arrive." In this word picture, we vividly see the power of energizing the emotional brain. The listener can empathize with the sense of loss—loss of feelings of security, or even the loss of hope.

Remember, to truly energize the emotional brain, give the listener a temporary feeling of loss. Then show how your solution provides relief from such painful feelings.

Principle: To ensure that audience members are moved to take action, connect with their emotional brain.

Power Questions: What parts of your speech get your audience to imagine potential loss? How can you make this experience vivid and then provide the salve—your solutions?

Part XII
Secrets about Networking:
Building Relationships and Winning
via the Internet

Networking and building relationships, utilizing the Internet, and working with the media are vital skills.

Powerful shortcuts to devising a strategy for interacting with the media and creating a compelling Web site are found in Personaltainment Branding™, which I revealed in my book *10 Seconds to Wealth*. Personaltainment Branding focuses on the P.E.C. Triangle. P.E.C. refers to personalized, entertaining and connecting.

- *Personalized* means you are important to me.
- *Entertaining* is giving the customer an enjoyable experience.

- *Connecting* helps fill the customer's empty feeling of loneliness.

An interviewer asked me, "Loneliness?"

I replied, "Yes. On some level, people feel alone with their problems. They want support and a feeling of connection."

To use Personaltainment Branding, take out your personal journal and note these questions to ask your listener.

Five Personaltainment Branding questions

1. What about this is working for you? (personalized)

2. When did this become fun for you? (entertaining)

3. What's most important about this for you? (personalized)

4. What has to happen in order for you to know that you have what you want? (connecting)

5. How can we make this work better for you? (connecting)

(Another version of the second question above is, "When could this become fun for you?")

When you design your Web site or media release around the Personaltainment Branding questions, your message becomes compelling. It gets people to take action that is favorable to you.

An interviewer asked me, "How do these questions make this happen?"

"It's about accessing people's emotions," I replied. "When you help people feel important and give them an enjoyable experience, they want to return again and again. For example, my buying experience through Amazon.com is quick, easy—and yes, for me it's fun. I love books, and hearing about what readers think about the book I'm considering. It is obvious that the creative team of Amazon.com has pre-planned ways to get readers enthralled. This is what I guide clients to do when they use the Personaltainment Branding questions as a springboard for designing Web pages and media releases."

How you can use the Internet for networking

Bestselling author Guy Kawasaki uses his blog to solidify relationships with his current customer base and with new people who come into his Web site via Google.com and other search engines. When I contacted Guy about this book, I knew what a fast-moving person he is. I suggested that he might repurpose something from his e-newsletter or his blog, which is titled *How to Change the World.*

So here is an excerpt from
Guy's Blog (blog.guykawasaki.com):

***Guest Article Below ***
October 25, 2007
A Night in the Life of Guy Kawasaki Plus Cool Stuff Friday
by Guy Kawasaki

It's 10:30 pm, and I'm sitting on a baggage cart on the tarmac of the Monterey, California airport. My U. S. Airways flight was set to depart and then an engine warning light went on—this was two hours ago. The reason we're all on the tarmac is that a fire alarm went off, so we had to evacuate the terminal.

Still, this is better than the last time I flew on U.S. Airways. That time one of the plane's engines died, and we made an "unscheduled stop" in Kansas City and then had to wait four hours for another plane to fly in. What's all of the got to do with this entry? Nothing except that I've had two hours to compile a short list of cool stuff.

It's been one of those days. This afternoon I spoke for my

buddies at Cisco [Systems]. Just before the speech, I discovered that the recently dry-cleaned pants that I packed were my son's, not mine, so I had to give the speech wearing jeans. One high point: Reggie Jackson was on the flight too, but he left after two hours of waiting. He was giving out autographs—though he didn't ask me for mine. :-) If I get to Las Vegas anytime soon, I'm speaking for the Entrepreneurs' Organization.

[On Guy's Blog, each of the below titles was an active link.]

"25 Tools to Compile an In-Depth Dossier on a Competitors' Site." This article contains description and links for you to scope out your competition's Web site. It covers topics such as ownership, traffic, links, trademarks, and browser compatibility.

"The Web Entrepreneur's Customer Service Toolbox: 100 Hacks and Resources." This is a compilation of useful tools and services to maintain a high-level of customer service. These tools help you keep in touch, run meetings, do accounting, provide support, and solicit feedback.

MeVu. This site enables you to create a page of links to all your Web presences. This means that people can go to one location for your profiles on Facebook, MySpace, and LinkedIn; pictures in Flickr and PhotoBucket; videos in YouTube; and musings in multiple blogs. Here is a sample. [Guy had a link here].

Catalog Choice. This is a not-for-profit that helps you reduce the amount of tree-killing, dump-filling, money-wasting catalogs that you receive (19 billion catalogs are printed each year in the U. S.). You denote which catalogs are coming to you, and Catalog Choice tells the companies to back off. It's a free service.

Best Book Combo. The site searches the catalogs of

AbeBooks.com, Amazon.com, BetterWorld.com, and Alibris.com and determines the best total price (that is, including shipping and handling) of a book. For example, the AbeBooks price for [Guy's book] *The Art of the Start* was $17.54 compared to Amazon.com's $18.20.

[Guy's blog is filled with links so that his readers can gain lots of valuable information fast!]

Guy Kawasaki is the chief evangelist of Canva, an online graphic design tool. He is on the board of trustees of the Wikimedia Foundation, a brand ambassador for Mercedes Benz USA, and an executive fellow of the Haas School of Business (UC Berkeley). He was also the chief evangelist of Apple. He is also the author of *The Art of the Start 2.0, The Art of Social Media, Enchantment,* and nine other books. Kawasaki has a BA from Stanford University and an MBA from UCLA as well as an honorary doctorate from Babson College. www.GuyKawasaki.com

More methods for working with the Internet
If you want to build a ship, don't herd people together to collect wood and don't assign them tasks and work, but rather teach them to long for the endless immensity of the sea.
– Antoine De Saint Exupery

Antoine's comment inspires us to touch people's hearts and create a feeling of longing in them. The old journalistic comment is, "If it bleeds, it leads." We notice that news broadcasts often begin with intense stories about hurricanes and other calamities.

If you can show people how to protect themselves from some kind of loss, you can seize their attention.

Perfection is achieved, not when there is nothing more to add, but when there is nothing left to take away.
– Antoine De Saint Exupery

Simplicity counts. We live in a sound bite culture. You need to get your message down to a simple, clear, hard-hitting point. "Your brand is the shortest distance to trust," I advised the audience of my sixth annual presentation to the National Association of Broadcasters Conference, in Las Vegas.

Here's how you can use the Internet and the media to create more profit. We will use the acrostic B.R.A.N.D.:

B - Begin with questions
R - Reveal stories
A - Alert to benefits and loss
N - Nurture relationships
D - Dig for information

Begin with Questions

How do you make your brand stand out and compel people to take action? Design your Web site to answer the questions a first-time Web visitor has in mind. In my speech *Online Secrets to Build Your Brand,* I revealed those questions:

- Who are you?
- How can you help me?
- How can you show me that you're trustworthy?
- Why must I take action now? (e.g., click on a hyperlink)

Ensure that your Web site includes your name, a moniker (such as "Success Coach"), and powerful testimonials to your trustworthiness. Use hyperlinks that identify how you help (for example, "increase your profit"). Remember, people don't buy services. They buy solutions.

As I mentioned earlier, use Personaltainment Branding™, make sure that your interaction with the Web visitor is personalized, entertaining, and connecting (what I call the P.E.C. Triangle). Design your Web site based on answers to these questions:

1. What about this is working for you (the Web visitor)? (personalized)

2. When did this become fun for you? (entertaining)

3. What's most important about this for you? (personalized)

4. What has to happen in order for you to know that you have what you want? (connecting)

5. How can we make this work better for you? (connecting)

Related to the first, third and fifth questions ("fun," "most important for you," and "make this work better for you"), a good example of Web design is found in Nightingale-Conant's Web site, which includes a computer-designed Personal Mission Statement that you create by typing in your own answers. For the third question ("most important to you"), effective Web marketers have designed hyperlinks to lure Web visitors.

Oprah.com's hyperlink, "Get Better Sleep," is enticing.

Reveal Stories

Many years ago, when she first coached me, author Dottie Walters impressed me with her stories. I always remember how vividly she conveyed her beginnings. She talked about placing cardboard in her shoes to cover the holes and using pillows to convert a one-seat stroller into a two-seat stroller, which allowed her to take her children with her to an important meeting.

Dottie energized me to feel that I could start from where I was and climb the staircase of success.

Now I use attention-grabbing stories: "When I was hanging by my fingertips to the hood of a speeding truck, I wasn't thinking about the movie cameraman capturing the stunt. I was only concerned about ... " About what? This is the element of a good story. The reader needs to respond, "What happened then?" This leads us to the use of a personal brand in building your Web site. Mark Victor Hansen's personal brand is "The Master of Mindset." My personal brand is "Executive Coach and Spoken Word Strategist."

Use your personal brand with well-chosen phrases on your Web site, in your e-mail and e-newsletters. For example, depending on the context I use: "I'm known as Executive Coach and Spoken Word Strategist because I help clients and audiences create a Wow! experience so their clients buy and they get breakthrough results ... In fact, Jaclyn Freitas, a meeting planner who booked me said, 'Using just one of Tom's methods, I got more done in 2 weeks than in 6 months.'" ... "Tom Marcoux coached me to get more done in 10 days than other coaches in 2 years." – Brad Carlson, CEO, Mindstrong LLC

Alert to Benefits and Loss

What reliably gets a Web visitor to click on a hyperlink? Alert the person to a potential loss. Fear of loss will get people to take action. To build your brand and sell items through the Internet, always include a deadline.

On a Web page that offers a product, begin with the product's benefit. Then point out how the person will lose without the benefit this product offers. The reason for this sequence is that if the first detail emphasized loss, a positive person might be turned off. However, when the first point is the benefits that are offered, a person who is loss-oriented will just read past those benefits, then key into the loss and buy your product.

Nurture Relationships

Build your brand online by creating a harmonious dance between your e-newsletter and a special-target Web page. For example, I wrote an e-mail message to be sent by persuasion expert David Barron to his list of thousands of subscribers. My e-newsletter message began, "I never expected to write *Darkest Secrets of Persuasion Masters: How to Protect Yourself and Turn the Power to Good*. But I was angry and I had to stand up for you."

I begin a relationship with the reader: "I had to stand up for you." I tell the truth about getting angry, and the reader sees me as a real human being. But this is not my usual positive way of communicating, so a few lines later I add, "This Darkest Secrets material is so intense that I am only releasing it with my most uplifting books: *Emotion-Motion Life Hacks* and *Relax Your Way Networking*.

The reader can then click to a specific Web page that includes the same information.

Please note: I reveal that I stand up for the reader; I'm a real person; and I provide helpful material to protect the reader.

Dig for Information

Effective Web marketers learn about their Web visitors. One method is to offer two free e-books and see which title pulls. Stay open to feedback. I named my Web site TomSuperCoach.com because a television host asked, "How do you spell Marcoux?"

When I interviewed Carly Fiorina (former CEO of Hewlett-Packard), she said, "You need to find the people who believe as you do. They're out there." The secret is to reinforce your brand by making your Web site, e-newsletter and business card tell the same compelling story.

Remember to tell *yourself* an empowering story. An old phrase holds "My prosperity prospers others."

Along this line, here's guidance from Jeanna Gabellini.

Why Clients Aren't Paying You What You're Worth
by Jeanna Gabellini

Darn near everyone gripes about money. I do it, too. We each have triggers about making, spending and saving money. But the one I hear the most about is not getting paid enough. Either you have an abundance of clients but they don't pay you for the real value you give or you don't have enough clients and you're scared to charge what you deserve.

You might not even know what you deserve because you've been brainwashed to take what you can get even if you only end up making twenty bucks an hour in the end. Maybe a few people gave you feedback that they can't afford your services and products and now you're convinced that nobody will buy at your current prices.

There are more than a few reasons why your ideal customers don't pay you what you're worth and it's not because they can't afford you! Think about it. If they're your ideal customers, then they see the value in what problem you solve and joyfully say *"yes"* to whatever price you set.

If you're not charging enough you may need to:

1. Figure out the real cost of doing business. Include all overhead and time spent for every little aspect of delivering each product and service.

2. Nail down exactly what you need to take home each

week.

3. Be more objective about the value your products and services give.

4. Lay out, on paper, the features and benefits of each product and service.

5. Charge from knowing what you want to grow into, not who you've been.

6. Consider yourself more of an expert in your field, even if you're a newbie. You bring something special to the table, no matter what stage of business growth you're in. When I was in coaches' training I was serving up breakthroughs for my "practice" clients long before I got my first paying client.

If your prices seem congruent with the value your products and services deliver, and not enough people are buying, you may need to:

1. Nail down your *ideal* customer and stop marketing and saying "yes" to those who don't fit that description.

2. Look at your beliefs about success, struggle, wealth and making a profit from what you love doing most.

3. Check in about what you offer. Do you love what you offer and the way you serve it up? How does your business support your desired lifestyle?

4. Clearly lay out the benefits and features of what you offer on all marketing materials. If you don't have bullet points on sales pages or brochures you probably aren't spelling it out clearly.

5. You're trying too hard to get clients. Pushing, needing, and worrying about getting money in the door comes from a place of lack and won't yield an abundance of anything (except heartache).

6. Tap into your Inner Business Expert and ask, "How can I align with more ideal customers? What should I shift? Is

there an action that would serve me in this desire?"

There are more than enough people out there to pay you what you are worth. Before you go killing yourself to try a bunch of new strategies to figure out how to attract them, sit with the suggestions above and feel into which ones may be perfect for you to put into action. One baby step at a time will be sufficient.

When it comes to client attraction it always starts with your beliefs. More than likely, you need to expect more. Make bigger financial goals and play to win. Play with confidence. Abundant expectancy without expectation.

Jeanna Gabellini is a Master Business Coach who assists conscious entrepreneurs to double (and even triple) their profits by leveraging attraction principles, proven strategies and fun. Grab her FREE audio on dialing in your biz at http://masterpeacecoaching.com/freecd

A FINAL WORD AND
SPRINGBOARD TO YOUR DREAMS

Congratulations on your efforts as your worked with the material in this book. To get even more value from this book, take the plans and insights that you created and place them in some form in your calendar or day planner. *Plan and take action.* Return to these pages again and again to reconnect with the material and take your life to higher levels.

The best to you,

Tom

Tom Marcoux
Executive Coach - Spoken Word Strategist

Special Offer Just for Readers of this Book:

Contact Tom Marcoux at tomsupercoach@gmail.com for special discounts on **coaching**, books, workshops and presentations. Just mention your experience with this book.

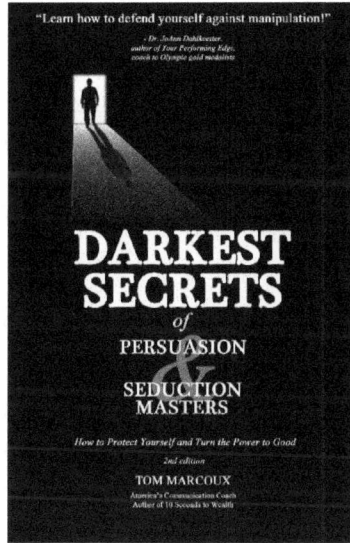

"Learn how to defend yourself against manipulation!"
- Dr. JoAnn Dahlkoetter,
author of Your Performing Edge,
coach to Olympic gold medalists

DARKEST SECRETS *of* PERSUASION & SEDUCTION MASTERS

How to Protect Yourself and Turn the Power to Good

2nd edition

TOM MARCOUX
America's Communication Coach
Author of 10 Seconds to Wealth

Excerpt from

Darkest Secrets of Persuasion and Seduction Masters: How to Protect Yourself and Turn the Power to Good

by Tom Marcoux, Executive Coach – Spoken Word Strategist
Copyright Tom Marcoux

. . . Now, I am in my 40's, with gray in my hair, and for 27 years I have been taking action to protect people.

And now is the time for me to protect you with the Countermeasures I reveal in this book.

Every human being needs to be able to break the trance that a Manipulator creates.

You need to make good decisions so you are safe and you keep growing—and you are not cut down and crippled.

This Darkest Secrets material is so intense that I first released it only with the counterbalance of my most energizing and uplifting books, *Nothing Can Stop You This Year!* and *10 Seconds to Wealth: Master the Moment Using Your Divine Gifts.*

An interviewer asked me: "Who can be the Manipulator?"

A co-worker, a boss, a salesperson, someone you're dating, and someone you think is a friend.

Now is the time—this very minute—for me to write this book to protect you.

I must speak the truth.

These Darkest Secrets of "persuasion masters" are …

Wait a minute! Let's say it plainly: These are the Darkest Secrets of masters of manipulation. Throughout this book, I will call these people what they are: Manipulators.

Dictionary.com defines "manipulate" as "To influence or manage shrewdly or deviously…. To tamper with or falsify for personal gain."

In this book, we will look on a manipulator as one who deviously influences someone with no concern about that person's well-being, and who causes harm to that person.

Here is the first Darkest Secret:

Darkest Secret #1:
Manipulators Make You Hurt
and Then Offer the Salve.

Manipulators would invite you to go out in the sun for hours and then sell you the salve to soothe your burns. The problem is that we don't notice that this is what they're doing.

For example, you're considering the purchase of a house. A Manipulator asks the question, "So, where would you put your TV?" This question is designed to put you into a trance.

Dictionary.com defines "trance" as "a half-conscious state, seemingly between sleeping and waking, in which ability to function voluntarily may be suspended." Let's condense this: in a trance you may not be able to function freely.

Here is the second Secret:

Darkest Secret #2:

Manipulators Put You into a Trance.

To protect yourself, you must learn to use Countermeasures to Break the Trance.

All the Countermeasures (actions you can take to break the trance) in this book will make you stronger and more capable of protecting yourself.

Now, we'll view the third Secret:

Darkest Secret #3:

Manipulators Care Nothing for You and Human Decency: They'll lie, cheat, and do whatever they need to do so they win—but their charm masks all this.

Let's return to the example of a Manipulator selling you a house. A Manipulator does not pause for an instant to see if you can truly afford the new house. The Manipulator would neglect to mention that you will not only have your mortgage payment of $900. There will be additional costs: home repairs, property tax ...

End of Excerpt from

Darkest Secrets of Persuasion and Seduction Masters: How to Protect Yourself and Turn the Power to Good

Purchase your copy of this book (paperback or ebook) at Amazon.com or BarnesandNoble.com
See **Free Chapters** of Tom Marcoux's 35 books
at http://amzn.to/ZiCTRj

ABOUT THE AUTHOR

You want more and better, right? Imagine fulfilling your Big Dream.

Tom Marcoux can help you—in that he's coached thousands of people: CEOs, small business leaders, graduate students (at Stanford University) speakers, and authors.

Marcoux is known as an effective **Executive Coach** and **Spoken Word Strategist.**

(and Thought Leader—okay, writing 35 books helped with that!)

** *CEOs, Vice-Presidents, Other Executives, Small Business Leaders:*

You know that leading people and speaking at your best can be tough.

Marcoux solves problems while helping you amplify your own Charisma, Confidence and Control of Time.

Interested? Email Marcoux—tomsupercoach@gmail.com

Ask for a *Special Report:*

* 9 Deadly Mistakes to Avoid for Your Next Speech

** *Speakers, Experts - for a great TED Talk, Book, Audio Book, Speeches, YouTube Videos.*

Marcoux solve problems while helping you to make your

Concise, Compelling Message that gets people to trust you and get what you're offering (product, service, *an idea*).

Yes - the *San Francisco Examiner* designated Tom Marcoux as "The Personal Branding Instructor."

Marcoux is an expert on STORY. He won a Special Award at the EMMY AWARDS, and he directed a feature film that went to the CANNES FILM MARKET and earned international distribution.

(Marcoux helps you *Be Heard and Be Trusted* . . . that's his 15th Anniversary, 3rd edition book.)

As a CEO, Marcoux leads teams in the United Kingdom, India and the USA. Marcoux guides clients & audiences (IBM, Sun Microsystems, etc.) in leadership, team-building, power time management and branding. See Tom's Popular BLOG: www.TomSuperCoach.com

Specialties: coach to CEOS * Executives * Small Business owners * Leaders * Speakers * Experts * Authors * Academics

One of his *Darkest Secrets* books rose to #1 on Amazon.com Hot New Releases in Business Life (and in Business Communication). A member of the National Speakers Association for over 14 years, he is a professional coach and guest expert on TV, radio, and print.

Marcoux addressed National Association of Broadcasters' Conference six years running. With a degree in psychology, Tom is a guest lecturer at **Stanford University**, DeAnza, & California State University, and teaches business communication, designing careers, public speaking, science fiction cinema/literature and comparative religion at Academy of Art University. He is engaged in book/film projects *Crystal Pegasus* (children's) and *Jack AngelSword* (thriller-fantasy). See Tom's well-received blogs

at www.BeHeardandBeTrusted.com

at www.YourBodySoulandProsperity.com

Consider engaging **Tom Marcoux as your Executive Coach.**

"As Tom's client for many years, I have benefited from his wisdom and strategic approach. Do your career and personal life a big favor and get his books and engage him as **your Executive Coach.**" – Dr. JoAnn Dahlkoetter, author of

Your Performing Edge and Coach to CEOs and Olympic Gold Medalists

"Tom Marcoux coached me to get more done in 10 days than other coaches in 2 years." – Brad Carlson, CEO of MindStrong LLC

Tom Marcoux can help you with **speech writing** and **coaching for your best performance.**

As Tom says, *Make Your Speech a Pleasant Beach.*

Join Tom's Linkedin.com group: *Executive Public Speaking and Communication Power.*

At Google+: join the community "Create Your Best Life – Charisma & Confidence"

Get a **Free** report: "9 Deadly Mistakes to Avoid for Your Next Speech and 9 Surefire Methods" at

http://tomsupercoach.com/freereport9Mistakes4Speech.html

Tom Marcoux has trained CEOs, small business owners, and graduate students to speak with impact and gain audiences' tremendous approval and cooperation. *Learn how to present and get thunderous applause!*

"Tom, Thanks for your coaching and work with me on revising my speech at a major university. Working with you has been so enlightening for me. Through your gentle prodding and guidance I was able to write a speech that connects with the audience. I wish everyone could experience the transformation I have undergone. You have helped me discover the warm and compelling stories that now make my speech reach hearts and uplift minds. This was truly an empowering experience. I cannot thank you enough for your great assistance." — J.S.

"Tom Marcoux has been an NAB Conference favorite [speaker] for six years. And he is very energetic."

– John Marino, Vice President, National Association of Broadcasters, Washington, D.C.

"Using just one of Tom Marcoux's methods, I got more done in 2 weeks than in 6 months."

– Jaclyn Freitas, M.A.

Tom's Coaching features innovations:

- Dynamic Rehearsal
- Power Rehearsal for Crisis
- The Charisma Advantage that Saves You Time

Become a fan of Tom's graphic novels/feature films:

- Fantasy Thriller: *Jack AngelSword*
  type "JackAngelSword" at Facebook.com
- Science fiction: *TimePulse*
  www.facebook.com/timepulsegraphicnovel
- Children's Fantasy: *Crystal Pegasus*
  www.facebook.com/crystalpegasusandrose

See **Free Chapters** of Tom Marcoux's 35 books
at http://amzn.to/ZiCTRj   Amazon.com
Your Notes:

www.ingramcontent.com/pod-product-compliance
Lightning Source LLC
Chambersburg PA
CBHW060611210326
41519CB00014B/3627